Custom Built

By Harley Davidson

North American Travels

By

Warren C. Garrison

With

Vivian Zanini

Ralph Garrison

Florence Blakey

Copyright © 2009 by Vivian L. Zanini

All rights reserved. No part of this book shall be reproduced or transmitted in any form or by any means, electronic, mechanical, magnetic, photographic including photocopying, recording or by any information storage and retrieval system, without prior written permission of the publisher. No patent liability is assumed with respect to the use of the information contained herein. Although every precaution has been taken in the preparation of this book, the publisher and author assume no responsibility for errors or omissions. Neither is any liability assumed for damages resulting from the use of the information contained herein.

ISBN 0-7414-5628-1

Published by:

INFINITY
PUBLISHING.COM

1094 New DeHaven Street, Suite 100
West Conshohocken, PA 19428-2713
Info@buybooksontheweb.com
www.buybooksontheweb.com
Toll-free (877) BUY BOOK
Local Phone (610) 941-9999
Fax (610) 941-9959

Printed in the United States of America
Published October 2009

Table of Contents

Introduction, by Vivian Zanini — vii

Chapter 1, The Ladder — 1

Chapter 2, Alaska, My last Frontier — 3

Chapter 3, Cross Country Adventuring — 19

Chapter 4, Incident at Spirit Lake — 34

Chapter 5, Canadian Trivia — 37

Chapter 6, On Little Loon Lake — 42

Chapter 7, Lower Forty-Eight — 44

Intermission — 65

Chapter 8, Coast to Coast — 66

Chapter 9, Westward Ho! — 82

Chapter 10, Highlights from the Oregon/California Trail — 87

Chapter 11, This is My Country, Land that I Love — 117

Chapter 12, The Last Ride Vivian Zanini — 128

Afterword, Footprints — 133

Acknowledgments 139

For Warren, I-8 to Yuma 141

Yuma 143

Acadiana in Louisiana 147

Journal Connections, by Ralph L. Garrison 150

The Elbert Farm 154

Chronicle of a Boy, a Dog, and a Tractor 158

A Letter to Warren, by Florence Blakey 165

Dedication to

Warren C. Garrison

Born August 1, 1930 in Topeka Kansas. Passed away July 1, 1992 in Anchorage, Alaska. On July 7, 1992, Warren's ashes were interred with full military honors at Fort Richardson National Cemetery near Anchorage. In lieu of flowers, he requested that donations be made to the American Cancer Society. That request is still valid. He was a right honorable man and a gentle spirit. We love him.

This dedication is by his siblings, Vivian, Ralph, Florence and posthumously, Phyllis, who made sure we have his photo.

Introduction

by Vivian Zanini

In the summer of 1990 when Warren came to see me in Torrance, California, he told me he had chronicled his adventures on the Harley that carried him the length and breadth of our North American Continent. The big tour bike had been custom built for him by Harley Davidson. That was engraved in gold on the gas tank. Hesitantly, he asked if I would read his journal, which I was privileged to do. Not being one to impose, he said he would like it if I ghost wrote it for him to 'flesh it out.' He wanted it to sound like some of his favorite books, suggesting Reader's Digest's "Off The Beaten Path," Charles Kuralt's "On The Road" and "On The Road Again," and magazines like "American Roads," "Arizona Highways" and "Scenic Byways" and was disappointed in his own writing ability. I assured him that it was beautifully done and needed no embellishment from me. Besides, I am a writer of fiction, I said, but I would be more than happy to type it up for him. The story was his and should remain that way. He remarked that non-fiction was the basis of fiction.

At that time he didn't leave it with me. More was to be written. He would be riding again in the summer of 1991 and beyond. He would send it to me when his travels around the country were complete, and again expressed the desire that I give it more storyline, more 'punch.' I said I'd see.

The mesothelioma cancer that had been in remission for almost a year, returned with a vengeance and was racing through his body like pac man. He wrote to me, during that winter of 1990-91, filling in his research on the places he had intended to travel the following summer. He asked if I would consider fulfilling his dream of riding in the great Southwest. Extensive reading and research about the physical geography and history of the territory around Yuma below the Colorado Plateau enchanted him. The voices of the old Colorado River gods called to him, he said, and his spirit yearned to see his favorite river from beginning to end. The beginning he had seen, the end he had not.

He did ride briefly in the fall of 1991, but only to see his siblings for one last time. From Los Angeles, he flew home to Alaska. He asked again, that I take his journal and do something with it. He had left it at our sister Florence's place in Missouri, still on his big motorcycle. I promised I would have her get it to me and she did. When we went together to say goodbye to him in Anchorage, she brought me the journal. I told him I had it and once more he requested that I 'spice it up' a little, and finish with the research letter he had written to me of Lake Charles, Louisiana and Darlington, Oklahoma. And if at all possible, would I explore the terrain around Yuma and travel the Colorado River from Yuma to the bottom of the Grand Canyon? I promised I'd try.

CUSTOM BUILT BY HARLEY DAVIDSON is built on the bones of Warren's journal. The ladder and corridor are as he described them to me.

I will do my best to stay in the company of "On the Road" as I translate his story.

Chapter 1

The Ladder

That pesky ladder again. Almost every time I triggered the morphine drip, it propped itself smack in the middle of my bed. I put my hand out to grab it, to make sure it was really there. But as usual, it stayed just out of reach.

Vivian sat in the corner, leafing through a National Geographic. "Sis," my voice was little more than a whisper, "is there a ladder on my bed?"

"Do you see a ladder, Warren?"

"I see it, but I'm not sure it's real."

She didn't seem surprised. "If you see it, it's real. Where does it go from your bed?"

"Into the ceiling I guess. I can't tell for sure."

Vivian smiled and raised her eyebrows. "Jacob's ladder?"

"Maybe. The morphine's kicking in." I closed my eyes, drifting into that no man's land of bizarre drug dreams. The same one came to trouble me again. I climbed the ladder and found myself in a long corridor. Doors, rows of doors on both sides, all closed. I was terrified that I would choose to open the wrong door.

This dream started plaguing me soon after the guy from hospice set up the drip for me. At first the ladder was just in that dream. Now it was showing up when I was awake.

Admittedly, a drowsy sort of awake, but at least aware of my surroundings. Propping itself up in the middle of my bed, it hovered there out of reach. I told Gundi, but she didn't want to hear about it. Just a morphine dream, she said, and put her arms around me to keep me safe. Finally, I was too weary to mess with it. Maybe Vivian was right. Maybe it was my ladder to wherever I was going. I hoped I'd open the right door.

This time, I got off the ladder and took a few steps down the corridor. The first door was locked and I breathed a sigh of relief. Just as I reached the second one, I heard the old familiar Harley Davidson trademarked idle sound '*sweetpotata-sweetpotata-sweetpotata*' way down at the end of the hall. My big, beautiful maroon tour glide Harley FLT stood there, motor running, headed into the very last opening. *"Custom Built for Warren C. Garrison by Harley Davidson."* The twenty-four karat gold letters on the gas tank glowed in the light shining from what was not a door at all, more like an adobe archway. I smelled chaparral and desert dust right after a sprinkle, sharp and fresh. Life DOES go on! I let out a whoop and ran toward my bike. *"Sweetpotata-sweetpotata-sweetpotata."*

Chapter 2

Alaska, My last Frontier

5-20-89

The sun rose on a beautiful day; clear and bright. It must be about 50°. Not having any responsibilities at home, I decided to ride up the Glenn Highway a ways. Today I rode alone. Often I ride on these short excursions with my motorcycle buddy, John, but today I needed to be alone with my big Harley. Yesterday, I had a treatment for the Mesothelioma that is compressing my lungs so relentlessly. The treatment is as painful as the disease. A long needle is jabbed into my pleural cavity and fluid sucked out. Fluid that is my body's attempt at accommodating the asbestos tumors growing there. Who knew, those years ago, how dangerous that stuff is? Sundance Wyoming, 1964 and the Air Force Nuclear power plant I, along with three other Military engineers designed. I taught myself calculus and nuclear physics to do that for the Army. We packed that hot radioactive core with layer after layer of asbestos. Now was payoff! My life was running out and I needed time on my motorcycle to fly down an easy highway with no helmet; to let the Alaskan wild winds sing along my shoulders, to face the inevitable end of life on Earth. I do so love this planet. We all know we must die, but not so often do we have the Angel of Death riding the handlebars right in front of us. When? A few months, a few years. Make it a few years. Like Robert Frost, I have "promises to keep and miles to go before I sleep."

The Glenn Highway follows the Matanuska River for its

entire length and is one of the most scenic routes in Alaska. My first stop was Sutton. I needed a short break from the fatigue of riding. An old Indian, probably an Athabascan, sat by the road in a broken down lawn chair, whittling on something and spitting tobacco on the ground all around him. I parked my bike and squatted down beside him. He spat on the opposite side.

"Nice day," I said to start some kind of exchange. He grunted "M-m," in response. "Lots of coal still lying around," I picked up a chunk and tossed it a few feet. That seemed to get him talking.

"You know about the coal days?" he squinted at me, his eyes lighting up a bit. "Lots of mining around here in the '20's and '30's. Even more during the Second war. Navy had a washing station here for a couple years, but then they went to oil, and since then the old station's rusted out. Mining was still important, though," he spat straight ahead. "There was Anchorage and the Army and Air Force bases needin' coal. But with the '50's came natural gas and that was the end of Sutton and the mining district. Now most everybody here commutes to Anchorage for work." He shrugged and spat on his boot, rubbing it in with a gnarled knuckle. Then he wiped the back of his hand on his Levis.

"Still lots of coal left, some of it Anthracite. 'Course there's coal all over Alaska. Just can't get to it by road."

"We got a sorta museum here if you'd like ta look." He hauled himself out of his seat and dug his chaw out of his lip and led the way to an old storefront that could have made a good movie set. Inside a display of mining and processing equipment was pretty well covered in a thick layer of dust. A photograph of a young moose in harness hung lopsided on the wall. Presumably he worked like a horse. He doesn't look too happy and I doubt the project was very successful. We left a trail of boot prints on the dusty planks when we walked out. I thanked the old fellow for the tour and shook his hand before I remembered the spit on it. Well, he wasn't likely contagious with anything worse than dirt. What did it matter anyway? So much for Sutton. I stretched to relieve the pressure on my lungs, ease the pain a little and get kinks out of my back. Time to ride on.

The highway parallels the Mat. That is the local short for Matanuska River. Some of the road is truly spectacular right now, running at water level then climbing to a high overlook carpeted with swaths of blue crocus and columbine and dotted with yellow daisies. Near the glacier, White Birch trees are coming into full leaf and Aspen are in bud. The air swirls heady scent of flowers and new growth. I breathe it in deeply.

The Mat Glacier is the source of this river; one of Alaska's most beautiful river/mountain glaciers. It is very clean and white with less detritus than most. Unfortunately, it has been receding for 10,000 years. As can be seen by its markings, at one time it extended all the way to Saltwater at what is now Anchorage, and stood several thousand feet tall at the snout, filling the entire valley. A river of ice some 90 miles long. Now it covers about 6 miles.

The mountains here are about 2500 to 5000 feet above sea level, which doesn't seem like much compared to the Colorado Rockies where I was raised, but the base of these mountains is essentially at sea level. They are as high above their base as the Rockies, but are steeper and more rugged. The upper third is still snow covered this late in the year. *Don't think about the Colorado Rockies right now.*

Mat Glacier has road access across private land and a fee is charged to use it. I dug in my pocket for some money. I had not gone far when I saw an old Army Jeep parked on the side of the gravel trail. The hood was up and a skinny kid with orange hair flagged me down.

"Hey, mister," he greeted me, "can I get you to hold this belt together while I duck tape it?"

I crawled off my Harley and walked over. "Duct tape? You hold the fan belt together with duct tape?" He must have been about 19 years old. His face was pocked with old acne scars and one ear was rimmed with studs and rings. His denims were Calvin Klein with torn out knees, obviously from Goodwill, but otherwise he wasn't bad looking.

"Do it all the time," he grinned engagingly, tearing a piece of tape off the roll. "About everything on this hunk of junk is held together with duck tape. Gets me around pretty good most of the time."

"Neat Harley you got there. Custom built, huh? Cost you a penny or two, I 'spect." He knew not to touch it. You don't touch another guy's Harley without permission.

I nodded. "Enough. Gets me around pretty good, most of the time." We laughed. "You been on the Glacier before?"

"Yeah," he rubbed his chin, "return visit. My folks brought me up here a while back. You know, when the 'enlightened' gathered during the conjunction of the planets to avert disaster. I was twelve, I think. I guess they were successful," he said sarcastically, "or if they hadn't sent up the good vibes, we'd all be cosmic soup by now. Thought I'd take a look at the old nut camp. Roll some weed, maybe, for old time sake. Hang out a while. You're welcome to come along," he invited "but you probably don't smoke pot."

"Probably not."

"Well, thanks for the help, mister. You're a cool dude." He climbed in his taped together jeep and roared off up the road. Cool dude? That shouldn't have ticked me off, but coming from an orange haired kid it did. His life had been no picnic either. Having flower children for parents could not have been an easy thing. He had a falling apart old Army Jeep had a custom built Harley tour glide FLT. He had thanked me for my help. *Be a cool dude, Warren. Let it go.*

I sat on my bike for a few minutes, looking up at Sheep Mountain. A herd of Dall Sheep grazed in a small glade, greening with waving grasses and drifts of purple fireweed flowers. This is a favorite place for the ewes to lamb in spring. Several caribou nibbled new grass along the road, very common here this time of year. And there, across the valley is Gunsight Mountain. When viewed from the east, it does bear a resemblance to an old notch type rear gun sight. Eureka Summit, rising 3822 feet, marks the division between the Mat River drainage and the Copper River basin. Bald eagles coast the wind currents here. Just for the joy of it. This is May. Life is happening all around me. Not just happening, but the earth has burst open and life gushes out, harsh and raw and splendid. It flairs out to all the senses. It fills the cones of my eyes with color; it streams fecund smells up my nostrils; it touches every part of my being, physical and non-physical. Distinctly I hear bees among the blooms, bleating lambs, bluebirds and robins singing to lure a mate, murmuring of the river, *sweetpotata-sweetpotata-sweetpotata.* I am alive. I am still here. But soon my body will lie among these glorious valleys and rugged mountains and the Aurora Borealis will wave stunning banners of colored light over its resting place. Here in my Beautiful Alaska. Land of the midnight sun.

The sun is getting low now. I'd best get back to Anchorage. I am exhausted from the ride and Gundi will be waiting dinner. Salmon fresh off the boat, she promised. She does a great baked salmon. We marry women to take care of them, and they end up taking care of us. Hell of a joke, Universe. I made a few hurried notes in my journal.

6-8-89

I rode to Homer today and ended up with a chipmunk in my saddlebag. Homer is about 250 miles southwest of Anchorage at the end of the Kenai Peninsula. It's a pleasant little town, picturesque in setting between mountains and sea and has a reputation for being an art center of sorts. Downtown are several good restaurants and souvenir shops. A local theater company puts on shows year round. It is something of a tourist town, being at the end of the road and has a fairly maritime Alaska atmosphere. Five mile long Homer Spit runs out where the waters at Kachemak Bay and Cook Inlet interact; reported to be the longest spit in the world. Homer is primarily a fishing village, halibut being the mainstay. They also take a lot of crab and lobster. Here too, coal was once mined, processed, and sold to the Navy. Quite a lot of coal lies on the surface, though none is being mined. Some of the locals pick it up for personal use. Saves on home heating bills.

I didn't really feel like staying in a hotel and mixing with the populace, so decided to camp at the city campgrounds located on a hillside overlooking the town and Kachemak Bay. I set up my tent next to a family who were loading up their RV to move out. They had a youngster, about 10 years old, I would judge. Nice looking kid. Brown eyes and dark curly hair. Something about him reminded me of myself at that age. He was bawling and arguing with his mother. Seems like he had captured a chipmunk and put it in a shoebox to take home. Naturally, Mom didn't agree with that and a conflict ensued. Feeling sorry for the kid, but understanding his mother's position, I went over to see if I could help.

"My name is Warren," I extended my hand to the mother. "May I talk to your boy?"

She smiled a bit thinly. "If you think you can help, go right ahead. I don't seem to be getting anywhere without being the evil witch. My son's name is Bobby."

I went over to the bench where he sat. "Hello, Bobby. Does your chipmunk have a name?" He wiped his nose on his sleeve, so I offered my handkerchief for his tears.

Glaring at his offending parent, he blew his nose loudly on the handkerchief and opened the box so I could see his bright-eyed trophy. "Yeah, I named him Chip."

What a surprise. "Well, I see you are from Nebraska, and Chip is used to Alaska. How about if I take him home with me, since I live in Anchorage, and my granddaughter can take care of Chip for you. Is that a deal?"

He thought about it for a minute. Since it was clear his mom was not about to give in and poor Chip would be left to survive on his own, he agreed that might work. "Thank you, sir," he said politely and held out his hand. Obviously the evil witch had taught him good manners. We shook hands on the deal and he handed over the shoebox and climbed into the RV. "Bye, Chip," he was still crying into my handkerchief.

I waved as the big RV from Nebraska drove away. Well, now I have a chipmunk to deal with. Maybe if I open the shoebox, Chip will decide to stay with his own family.

There is a park nearby and several baseball games in progress. I walked around for a few minutes, did controlled breathing and watched one of the games. Rain began gently and a heavy cloud cover hung overhead. I hoped it didn't get any worse. In fact, it would be nice if it got a little warmer than the 50° it is right now. Hazards of the bike traveler, I guess. You take what the weather gods hand out whether you like it or not.

The climate in Homer is usually a bit more pleasant than

most of South Central Alaska. In past years there was a lot of agriculture here, and it could easily be more productive and profitable from an economic point of view than it has become. At the moment, however, economy is in keeping myself and my bike and my chipmunk dry. I covered my Harley, lit my sterno burner in the tent and heated a can of beans. Chip decided to share with me, so I spooned some beans onto a piece of paper from my journal for him instead of letting him bury himself in the can I ate from. When he finished, he curled up in my denim jacket and went to sleep. I transferred him to his box, tucked one of my two towels around him and left the lid off. What have I got myself into? It's been a short day, but I'm too tired to take notes. I wish I had time and ability to write about my travels in Alaska, there is so much to tell. Maybe I can get Sis to do it for me if I keep notes. But right now I just need to sleep.

6-9-89

Chip woke me early this morning. Rain came off and on all night and I'm sure his nest was cozier in the box than in the woods, but it seemed reasonable that he would go out to forage at daylight. Dream on. Chip was not about to abandon a sure thing, so I shared my bacon and bread with him and packed my tent and gear to get on the road again. Well, Chip saw his opportunity and made one wild leap onto my Harley and snuggled into my bedroll. Seems I am going to have a traveling companion for the time being, so I tied on his box and we got on the way.

Anchor Point is a hamlet located about 20 miles north of Homer, the western most point of the North American Continent that can be reached by road. Until time runs out for me, it is my plan to crisscross ride from the farthest west to the farthest east points on the North American Continent, then do the same north and south to the Mexican border. I don't think I want to go farther south than that. But for a very long time, I have wanted to explore the great Southwestern US. Old stories of the Yuma Territory have tantalized me for years. So today I am at Anchor Point. Its main claim to fame is a sport fishing area. Sports fishermen from as far away as New Zealand take King Salmon here. Across Cook Inlet, you can see dormant volcanoes, Mt Iliamna and Mt Redoubt. Mt Augustine, also seen from here, is still active. North and a little east is the Kenai-Soldotna area. When Russia claimed Alaska, it established a primary settlement here. This, too, is another King Salmon fishing paradise, and Kenai-Soldotna is the site of the original oil discovery and development in the early 1960's.

At the junction of the Sterling Highway and the Seward Highway lies a small lake. Because it is a favorite nesting place for Arctic Terns, guess what it is called? Right. Tern Lake. Terns hold the world's record for long distance travelers. They breed and nest at Alaskan tundra ponds and lakes that have an almost unlimited supply of plants, insects and small animals for birds raising hungry chicks. In late summer, they fly with their young from the Artic to the Antarctic where Southern Hemisphere summer is just beginning to arrive. Round trip from Alaska to Antarctica and back is some 25,000 miles total. Other Arctic birds that commute long distance are the jaeger that spends its winter on the open Pacific near Japan, the plover that migrates to Hawaii or Argentina, and Tierra del Fuego at the tip of South America is the winter home of surfbirds. The Arctic warbler warbles the cold months away in Asia.

I share all this fowl information with Chip. He has finished his morning nap and is sitting on the back of my Harley, (ours now, I guess) and cheerily answers. Flipping around as if searching out any elusive birds that might consider him a handy meal, he jumps to my shoulder. Satisfied that he is secure on his present vehicle, he returns to the comfort of my bedroll (his bedroll?) and suggests we continue on.

On its way to Anchorage, the Seward Highway passes around the Turnagain Arm of Cook Inlet. Cook Inlet is named for the famous Captain Cook who explored this coastline before he was murdered in Hawaii. Turnagain Arm is known for its high tides and frequent bore tides. I have seen a bore tide here as high as 5 feet. Turnagain Arm and Knik Arm constitute the upper reach of Cook Inlet with Anchorage lying at their junction.

Portage Glacier is an interesting side trip from here and I consult with Chip about the feasibility of such a venture. He assures me he would relish it since he has never seen Portage Glacier. Actually, it is one of the most accessible of Alaska's many such frozen rivers. Sadly, it is receding quite rapidly. The Forest Service has a nice visitor's center here with good observation points and snack vending machines. The glacier foots a lake and dropping icebergs make a spectacular show from time to time. Chip fusses that he is getting a bit hungry, as am I, so I select the best looking of the shrink-wrapped sandwiches and a bag of pretzels and we sit on a bench to eat and watch for an iceberg to fall. I'm beginning to like the company of the little rascal sitting next to me. He is someone to talk to, someone to share my ride with. Not a bad deal after all.

By late afternoon we are home in Anchorage. I plan to take Chip into the woods behind our backyard, but Gundi thinks he's cute and makes up a fleece-lined bed in his shoebox. She thinks the back porch is a good place for it. A few years back I had a dog named Useless and Gundi folded his doggy door flap open a little so Chip could get out if he needed to 'go'. I asked whom she thought she was fooling, but he must have done it, because I never found his droppings or urine inside. Obviously he adopted our house as his own and eventually he was let into the kitchen. Any time I went into the garage, he was right there and leapt up on the FLT. If I chose another of my Harleys or the car or truck, he stayed in the garage until I got back and he never went with Gundi. But if I took my big Harley, he was along for the ride.

6-17-89

Today, Chip and I rode to Fairbanks via the Parks Highway. This is the newest road in Alaska, having opened to the public in October 1971. I first rode it in November 1971 when it was all gravel surfaced. A couple of years later, it was paved and is now one of the best roads in the state.

Willow is about 67 miles from Anchorage. In a referendum some ten years ago, voters attempted to move the capital from Juneau to Willow. That was very upsetting to politicians, of course, since it put them so much closer to and under more scrutiny from, the populace. Definitely not what they wanted, so they got a commission to come up with an astronomical cost of moving and put it to a vote again. This time the voters rejected the project because of the cost and the politicians won again. When I explained this to Chip, he raised such a ruckus I thought at first he had the same opinion of politicians as I did, but then I realized a huge raven was flapping around overhead. Apparently that was what raised his ire. Crows, politicians. What difference? Both are in it for the pickings.

Willow Creek is a salmon spawning stream and the King Salmon are just starting to run, so the fishermen are after them big time.

At about 100 miles, the highway crosses the Susitna, one of Alaska's major rivers. It rises in the Alaska Range and empties into Cook Inlet and is carrying a lot of water from the snowmelt right now. We have some really nice views of Mt McKinley along here. It's 20,320 feet above sea level and that makes quite a chunk of mountain. Originally this majestic mountain was called Denali, The Great One. The Athabascans said the mountain was created by a battle between two warriors. Raven war chief Totson chased his enemy Yako down a river, throwing his spear at his foe. Yako changed a gigantic wave to stone, which turned the spear from its course. The wave stone became the mountain. Denali is the name still used by locals and natives. It is the highest mountain in North America and technically could be the highest in the world. The north face of Denali rises almost 18,000 feet above its base, a gain in elevation that exceeds Mount Everest.

About 60 million years ago, two tectonic plates collided and elevated, producing such heat that sections of the earth's crust began to melt, and masses of molten rock solidified to granite. Eventually the uplift of granite wore down more slowly than the surrounding sedimentary rock. That granite is Denali. Another tectonic uplift began two million years ago and continues to the present day, giving The Great One its towering height.

Denali became known as McKinley by way of the gold standard. In 1896 William Dickey led an expedition prospecting for gold in an area south of the mountain. In camp, he argued with other miners whether US currency should be backed by gold or silver. He was for gold, the other miners for silver. When Dickey returned to the lower 48, he proposed that the highest mountain on this continent should be named for presidential candidate William McKinley, who championed the gold standard. McKinley won the election and the name was adopted. Chip was not duly impressed with all this information. Apparently he considered it so much malarkey. He was snuggled in my jacket pocket fast asleep, his tiny head barely visible under my arm.

Broad Pass is at about 200 miles. This is appropriately named; a broad and shallow pass through very old, much eroded, and no longer noticeable mountain range. It is interesting that immediately north of here is the young, high and still growing Alaska Range. The Nenana River rises on the south slope of the Alaska Range, but turns at Broad Pass and heads north where it has managed to find and maintain a channel through that range as it has grown. It shares this characteristic of a south flowing river running north with the Delta River about 200 miles east of here and a section of the Colorado River in Arizona's Grand Canyon. In this way, those three rivers are unique in the world.

We passed through Healy where I worked at the power plant for a couple of years (1970-71). At the time, it was the only pulverized coal burning plant in the State. I believe it still is. The area has built up quite a lot in the past 20 years. When we were here, the only habitations were trailers haphazardly scattered about. Now it is almost a town with many real houses.

Fairbanks is the second largest city in Alaska, with a population of about 50,000 and is the commercial center of the Interior and is a tourist Mecca in summer months when daylight lingers for 22 hours and temperatures average in the mid 60's and can reach as high as mid 90's. It's a different story in winter and few visitors venture to stay, with 3+ hours of sunlight each day, and the thermometer hovering at 30 below zero, although those magnificent Northern Lights are a saving grace. We lived in the Interior for 5 years before moving to Anchorage in late 1971. The University of Alaska Fairbanks (UAF) is home to a Large Animal Research Facility, formerly known as The Musk Ox Farm. These wooly prehistoric cattle share the research pastures with reindeer, caribou and moose. I assured Chip I would not leave him there, and we rode on to the "co-op" for a bite to eat at the diner. During construction of the trans-Alaska oil pipeline it was a beehive of activity and people from the villages still often eat there when they come to town. Sharing the blue plate special with a chipmunk didn't create much attraction. We rode the Harley on downtown past the Northward Building, the first steel-girded skyscraper built in the Interior. It was the inspiration for Edna Ferber's novel "The Ice Palace."

The oldest road in Alaska is the Richardson Highway. Originally a pack trail between the mining settlements of Eagle and Valdez, following the gold rush it extended to Fairbanks, linking the Interior to the ice-free port of Valdez. Today, the Richardson joins the Alaska (Alcan) Highway for 98 miles between Fairbanks and Delta Junction. Here too, is Fort Greely, where I was stationed from 1965 to 1969 and where I retired from the Army 20 years ago. The Tanana Valley in the delta area is the largest farming venture in the State. Imported from Montana in 1928, 23 buffalo were introduced as game animals. Maybe their ancestral shaggy bison that ranged here millennia ago have been spirit watchers, for that original herd has grown to number more than 400 and provided the source for other herds to be established elsewhere in Alaska. Even though they have been given their own extensive acreage along the Delta River, there is no way to keep them from wandering onto the nearby garden patch.

From Delta to Paxon is a very scenic ride. The road parallels the river for about 80 miles as it carves a path through the Alaska Range. The peaks here often tower 14,000 feet above a base of 1000 to 1500 feet. That is a lot of mountain. From Paxon we rode along the Gulkana River. The notorious Trans-Alaska pipeline passes through this area and frequently can be seen from the road. Environmentalists screamed long and loud, petitioned the government, and raised holy hell in general about this pipeline. It crossed the pathway of migrating reindeer and would cause them great anxiety. Eventually the compromise was to raise it on tripod frames to a height of four feet above ground, so the herds could pass under it. But as it turned out, the reindeer and caribou make good use of it. They stand on top and face into the wind, letting the nasty gigantic mosquitoes blow off their hides and out of their eyes. Then at night, they are on their way again. Good ecological bonus, that pipeline.

Some of the better-known roadhouse ruins can be found

along the Richardson Highway. At one time, Alaska had more than 3000 of these 'inns', which ranged from tents or dugouts to fairly decent log structures. Typically, walkers and teamsters using the trail planned to travel about 30 miles a day, so the roadhouses were located around 15 miles apart. For $2, a traveler got a hot meal, probably rabbit, moose, lynx, bear, or caribou stew, and for another $2, he and his dog team got a place to sleep for the night. That might be a space on the dirt floor to spread his bedroll.

Chip and I stopped at the Sourdough Roadhouse; I believe the only one still operating in the original building. Certainly not an imposing structure, still it is quite genuine and has lots of real atmosphere. Not an architectural design work, but unique in its own way. I bought a packet of pretzels for Chip, helped myself to the extensive buffet and took a small table in the far corner of the room so as not to bring too much attention to my dining companion. Who was I kidding? He was the star of the show and loved it.

The roadhouse at Black Rapids is still the original building, but it is closed now. Hopefully some enterprising soul will buy and restore it. At Delta is Rika's Roadhouse, one of the most famous. The two-story lodge has been restored and is operated by the State as a museum, gift shop and restaurant. A very elaborate place, a Finnish lady named Rika originally owned it. When I was stationed at Fort Greely in the Sixties, she was living in Delta. Her roadhouse was going to ruin, so it is good to see it restored and being used again. Only a few of the originals still survive as ruins along the 366 miles of Richardson Highway. Besides Rika's Roadhouse, The Sourdough Roadhouse, (which claims a sourdough starter dating back to 1896,) and Black Rapids Roadhouse are in use. Still standing are The Paxon Inn, The Sullivan Roadhouse and Meier's Lake Roadhouse. The present Copper Center Lodge is built on the site of the old Blix Roadhouse, a popular stop in the late 1800's. Along this route, a telegraph line, built by the US Army, ran from

Valdez. In the Sixties, still in place stood old telegrapher's shacks and even some of the wire swung from tripods on which the line suspended. Now, all that has disappeared.

Chip and I will head home to Anchorage tomorrow. In spite of extra padding on the Harley seat and frequent stops to stretch and breathe, the old body has taken quite a beating over the last few days. I must rest a week or so and get another cancer treatment before I head for the big summer ride. Maybe I can get some of the info from this ride into my journal while I recoup. I need to leave something of myself behind. My knowledge of Alaska. Alaska is an Aleut Indian word meaning "Great Land." Indeed.

Chapter 3

Cross Country Adventuring

7-5-89

We left Anchorage about noon today for a trip to the lower forty-eight. I asked Gundi to ride with me, as she has sometimes done before. She has a comfortable buddy seat on the FLT and fur wraps and boots when needed, but she says this is the best time of the year in Alaska, and decided to stay home. The weather has been unusually sunny and warm for the past couple of weeks, but this morning the temperature was down about 10° with a fine mist in the air. While I don't relish bike riding in rain, the mist isn't bad enough to stop me. I need to get on the road if I'm leaving today at all, and it is expected to clear later. I'll wear my helmet with the visor up for a while. Ordinarily in rain, that is a bad idea since I can't hear the sounds around me with a helmet. I do not like riding through states where helmets are mandatory. They can be as dangerous as not wearing one at all. More so, I believe. Would you drive a car with your head wrapped up and only a slit to see through? Look over your shoulder. Really? Pull over for a siren. What siren?

Thought maybe I should leave the chipmunk home with Gundi, but he snuggled down in one of the saddlebags. Little does he know the length of this trip. Could be he will like the Missouri country and decide to make his home there. In the meantime, he is someone to talk to. By 2 P.M. the sky cleared and it was back to being good again. I secured my helmet to the back of buddy seat and Chip squirted out of his nest and perched behind me for a while. Amazing how he can hang on to the leather seat back.

Palmer is 40 miles out of Anchorage on the Glenn Highway. Along this stretch is the Eklutna Village Historic Park, where St. Nicholas Russian Church is located. It is surrounded by "Spirit houses," a mixture of Native and Russian culture. I've lived in Anchorage for eighteen years, driven the Glenn Highway many times, but never taken the cutoff to see this relic of Alaskan history. It would take a little time off my schedule, but I was not on any particular timetable and Chip seemed agreeable with the idea.

The small church is constructed of hand-hewn logs and is probably the oldest building in the Anchorage area. The spirit houses clustered around it are a curious sight; brightly painted structures built over traditional graves. Most of them are in need of repair. I spotted a bicycle leaning on one of several picket fences and a girl working on one of the houses. She was probably about fifteen or sixteen years old, and definitely not a Dena'ina. Most of the natives here are Dena'ina Indians. This girl had white-blond hair, very fair skin and blue eyes. I asked her name and if she could tell me more about the little houses and what they meant. She said she was Kirstin and the one she was repairing and repainting was her great-grandmother's grave. She explained that before the Russians owned Alaska, the Athabascan Indians buried their dead and covered the grave with a blanket for 40 days, then built a spirit house over it and put in personal belongings the person might need for the next world. She herself was of Russian ancestry and so her family's spirit houses had picket fences around them to show they were not Native Indians. Kirstin pointed out a larger structure that she had finished painting and showed me a little one inside it. That was her mother's. If a small spirit house is built inside a larger one, a child is buried with its mother. I asked what had caused her mother's death. She frowned and said with a touch of bitterness, "Too many kids. I have 14 brothers and sisters and I'm the youngest. The last was one too many."

I speculated to myself what could have been the medical reason for such a death. Anchorage is not that far away and has good hospitals and doctors, yet her mother must have chosen to give birth at home. From the look of this daughter, her home was clean and relatively sanitary. Maybe it is possible to simply give out from childbearing too often.

Kirstin reached toward Chip who was perched on my shoulder. "May I hold him?" He did not object to a stranger's hands and seemed to warm away her anger.

I asked about the double crosses that stood at the foot of every spirit house. She said the upper bar of the Russian Orthodox Cross represents the sign, "INRI", Jesus of Nazareth, King of the Jews; the middle bar is where he hung, the left end of the slanted bar points up to heaven where the repentant thief went, and the right end points down to hell where the second thief resides. I wondered if Kirstin knew that similar crosses have been used for thousands of years by various cultures. The Egyptians, the Peruvian Indians and among others, the Anasazi, to whom it was the Raincross, representing the dragonfly that comes with summer rains. Burying personal items with the dead is not unusual in any culture. We all do it in one way or another.

She took me inside the church and showed me the altar. It is quite ornate with pictures and tapestries of saints. Candles burned on side altars and hand-woven rugs covered the floor. It all seemed out of place in the rundown church. Apparently someone cared enough to keep it up. Maybe it was this girl whose faith sustained her in this place.

I wished her good day and walked to the Harley. If Chip wanted to stay with her, it might be a good thing for both of them. But not to my surprise, he leaped out of her grasp and made a beeline for the buddy seat, perching upright and chattering at Kirstin as we drove away. Was he offering her understanding and peace? Who can say? The last I saw of her, she had returned to repairing her family spirit houses.

Palmer is where the Federal Government started up an agricultural colony in the 30's during the great depression. The purpose was to relocate destitute farmers from the dust bowl states, give them land and a new start. Of course, in its usual infinite wisdom and mismanagement, the government gave each farmer only 40 acres, far too little to do much with. But some of them stuck it out and eventually consolidated acreages into decent sized holdings. Kirstin's grandfather may have been one of these. Dairying hung on for a long time, but now it is gone. At the present time, most are truck gardening and small hay fields where moose hang out, and some hobby farms.

The Alaska State Fair is held in Palmer in late August to show off the produce that grows to such extraordinary size here due to the length of summer days. Blue ribbon minimum seventy-five pound cabbages in 19½ hour daylight, carrots, potatoes, and strawberries. Eat your heart out, California. This part of the Matanuska-Susitna Valley is called the breadbasket of south central Alaska.

Past Eureka Summit to Glennallen, the road passes through some relatively uninteresting country; rolling to hilly, covered with tundra and some areas of scrub spruce and aspen. Chip did not find this area uninteresting. He kept out of sight in my jacket pocket, scouting the sky for the abundant numbers of hawks and eagles and other birds of prey that inhabit this area. After several routine miles I looked in my rearview mirror and suddenly the road was interesting to me as well. Charging along behind me and closing fast was a large female moose. Whether she wanted to claim the Harley as her calf, or as a threat to her calf, I chose not to find out and increased my speed just enough to keep her coming, but not enough to lose her. After a few miles at this pace, she gave out and stood panting to catch her breath. I rounded a curve and lost sight of her, but the episode broke the monotony of the terrain for both the moose and me.

About 20 miles west of Glennallen and some 200 miles east of Anchorage, are some good views of Mt. Wrangell, an extinct volcano that stands pretty much alone at 14,000 plus feet above sea level. Glennallen is the headquarters for the Wrangell-St Elias National Park. This park was created in 1980 and is America's largest park, covering some 13.2 million acres. Some predictions are that is will become 'the next Denali' in terms of use by tourists.

The road from Glennallen to Tok is called the Tok Cutoff, built in the '40's to shorten the distance on the Alaska Highway between Tok and Anchorage. As noted in the previous journal entry, The Alaska Highway ends at Delta Junction where it connects with the Richardson Highway that runs from Valdez to Fairbanks. Much of it parallels the Copper River, so called for the rich deposits of copper in its drainage. Around the turn of the century, a copper deposit was discovered between the Kennicott Glacier and McCarthy Creek and became the Kennecott Copper Corp. Kennecott was misspelled in the naming, whether intentional or not, I don't know. When the mine closed in 1938, it had produced 4.5 million tons of ore, said to have been worth $200 million. The area has become a tourist haven with air-taxi operations to a hotel, B&B Inns, and the like.

The Copper River Valley has some subsistence farming, but is considered to have agricultural potential should the demand arise. The Tok cutoff passes through the Alaska Range. The mountains here are rugged and steep, but not nearly as high as the area of Mt. McKinley and Delta. Here the range starts to diminish and soon disappears to the east. In the opposite direction, the Alaska Range runs west from here to become the Aleutian Islands where it sinks below the surface of the

Pacific Ocean. The Kennicott and Root glacier runoff from Tok to near the border with Canada in the Wrangell Mountains, is headwaters of the Tanana River, the longest tributary of the Yukon at about 400 miles in length. The Tetlin Indian Reservation and the Tetlin Wildlife Preserve are found in this headwater country. Canada Customs is at Beaver Creek. It bills itself as the farthest west community in Canada. I picked up some rain here. All the campgrounds and motels are full. I stopped at the little all night café and bought a container of mutton stew. Probably made this morning, but at least hot and filling. I keep a bag of Wheaties cereal for Chip. That seems to be his favorite food. He likes it better than the chipmunk food sold at campground vending machines. I might share some with him for my dessert, but have no milk. Chip doesn't care for milk, but then neither do I. I'll pass on dessert for now and just dream about cherry pie alamode and a mug of hot coffee. We pitched my tent and made a soggy camp west of Chisana Creek, ate our late meal and crawled into my sleeping bag. It is midnight now and I feel well enough to write of our day. Chip is asleep under my pillow. Unusual for me to feel this good after such a long ride. I will sleep well and without pain.

My Harley's odometer reads 57,087 miles. We did 487 miles today.

7-6-89

Chisana, a few miles south of where we camped, was the site of Alaska's last gold rush in 1913. It lasted a brief two years. During that time period, around 10,000 people stampeded through the Chitistone and Skolai Pass routes. Now, fewer than 20 people live in Chisana year round. Kluane Lake is the largest lake in the Yukon Territory and prevailing winds get pretty chilly. It seems to me to always be cold here and doesn't really thaw until July. Between Chisana and this lake is truly spectacular country. The vast scale of things is remarkable, with rugged peaks, most unexplored. Here are rock faces over a thousand feet high, dozens of waterfalls and hanging glaciers with stunning "rock gardens" of immense lichen covered boulders. In spite of all the ice and snow, the valleys teem with life among the alder groves and flower-covered tundra. Dall sheep live on the rocks, moose and brown bear prowl the hills, ptarmigan, pikas, squirrels and robins can be found in the alders, and eagles soar above. Wildflowers paint the tundra meadows a mix of color like an impressionist artist's brush. Though this is a designated wilderness area, it is easily accessible by airplane and the last few years have taken a toll on its fragile environment with increased use by modern day explorers who refuse to stay on marked trails. Littering, a growing problem with bears that associate humans with free food, and trampling of vegetation are a major concern. It takes more than a hundred years for tundra to recover from a single footprint.

Between Kluane Lake and Haines Junction is an agricultural research station that is fairly active. Haines Junction in Canada connects with Haines in Alaska via the Alaska Highway that is known in the Yukon as Haines Highway, a distance of 150 miles. Haines is the end of the ferry line from Seattle and is a center for Tlingit Native art and dance. It is a favorite spot for king and sock-eye salmon fishing. In late fall, bald eagles come from hundreds of miles away to feast on a late run of salmon. 3000 or more eagles make this yearly "Bird Convention." Noisy, messy, stinky? Helmet and undercover chipmunk!

An old pipeline runs from Haines to Fairbanks. It is a four-inch line that carried fuel for Military installations in Alaska, but it was shut down in the late sixties. Old Fort William Henry Seward is south of Haines. The 19th Century officers' homes and command buildings are still in use; two homes are a hotel and the Alaska Indian Arts Center is in another. Alaska does not waste resources. Reuse, reduce, recycle.

At Beaver Creek Customs we pass into Canada and points south. Whitehorse is the capital of the Yukon Territory. It was built when The White Pass & Yukon Route Railroad narrow gauge line was completed from Skagway to Whitehorse in 1900, a distance of 100 miles, to carry supplies to miners. From the Whitehorse terminal, these supplies went by riverboat to Dawson City, then the capital of the Territory, and from there by packhorse to the gold fields. The railroad followed the old White Pass Trail, known as "Dead Horse Trail', for the 3000 pack animals that perished in the rugged canyon. In the early 1980's the railroad closed down, but reopened in 1988. Tourists who take the train from Skagway to Fraser along the cut in the mountainside, can see the remains of many of the old trails hundreds of feet below. From Fraser, they take a bus to Whitehorse. On the opposite side of the canyon, the drive along the Klondike Highway between Skagway and Whitehorse has much the same scenery; Pitchfork Falls, Skagway River Gorge, and beautiful lake country. Miles Canyon is immediately upstream from Whitehorse and dangerous rapids were among many hazards that faced would-be gold miners as they floated downstream from Dawson. I understand, though, that these rapids were nothing compared to the famous Whitehorse Rapids that claimed so many lives. At the turn of the century, "white horse" was the common term for whitecaps, or whitewater, thus the name Whitehorse Rapids. These rapids are no more. They are covered by the reservoir that provides electricity to the town. About 20 miles upstream is Marsh Lake, which gives rise to the Yukon River. At 2000 miles long, it is one of the longest rivers on the North American Continent. One can travel on this river from Whitehorse to the Bering Strait.

Whitehorse became the capital of the Yukon Territory in 1953 with a population of over 20,000 and is the third largest city in Canada by area. It boasts several interesting historical things, such as an old sternwheeler riverboat, the SS Klondike that operated until the '50's. It is on the registry of

Historical Sites. In 1974, two other sternwheelers, the Casca and the Whitehorse, burned up in a fire. Whitehorse claims the world's largest weather vane at the airport. Actually, it is a graceful old DC-3 on a pedestal built by Al Jacobs, a welding engineer. Due to a fine balance point, she always points into the wind. A 5-knot breeze is enough to turn her. She boasts a colored history of honor to disrespect and back again. Since it was still early in the afternoon and I intended to spend the night here, I got a motel room for Chip and myself and headed to the airport to further research this unique airplane's past.

Douglas serial number 4665 was built in 1942 and served for three years in USAAF camouflage colours, flying transport in China and India. In 1946, the Canadian Pacific Airlines bought a fleet of C-47's and the DC-3 was sold as part of that fleet. Converted to civilian configuration with passenger seating for 28, she was issued Canadian registration CF-CPY. I read this to Chip from a plaque, and found a book to take back to our room to read further. Apparently, CF-CPY as she is called, flew CPA scheduled routes throughout Canada during the 1950's. When CPA upgraded their aircraft fleet, CF-CPY was downgraded to fly domestic runs between Whitehorse and mining towns. In 1960, Connelly-Dawson Airways acquired the faithful old lady and for six years she wore skis or wheels as a bush plane, hauling supplies to remote locations. In 1966, she again flew out of Whitehorse on charter routes of Great Northern Airways until 1970, when GNA went bankrupt. Though Northward Airlines bought her with a total flying time of 31,851 hours, she never flew again, and was used for parts until she was donated to the Yukon Flying Club in 1977. Fortunately, the club restored this veteran aircraft to the CPA colors of her glory days, intending to display her permanently at the Whitehorse airport. The restoration took four years, then she was raised onto her present pedestal, a truly fitting place for such a grand old airplane.

I read this while Chip and I ate our supper in a nice restaurant finished off with cherry pie alamode and a mug of hot, fresh coffee. I shared a couple of cherries with my chipmunk, then we retired to our motel room for the night. The Harley odometer reads 57,354 miles. We logged a short 267 miles today, but got some sightseeing done.

7-7-89

We left Whitehorse about ten o'clock this extraordinarily beautiful morning. Temperature at 70°, calm wind and clear sky that boded no rain made me happy, since riding my bike in wet weather is not particularly pleasant. Most of the drive from Whitehorse to Watson Lake is rather unremarkable, though I understand it is great country for bird watching. I did enjoy seeing the occasional brilliant color of bluebirds flash by, and several flocks of Canada Geese grazed near the lake. As usual in these circumstances, Chip kept himself well hidden in the denim jacket that I strap on the back of my seat. He cuddled in the folds with his head sticking out, but easily withdrew from sight when he spotted an owl or hawk.

Watson Lake is a small town founded by Frank Watson, a prospector and trapper, around 1903. Originally from California, he was the first white man to travel over land to this area. Later, he moved his family a few miles north as more people came to settle here. He died of pneumonia in route to Fort St John medical facilities via mail plane. His children and grandchildren are still a predominate influence in the community. Watson Lake is about the middle of the Alaska Highway. It was used as an accommodation and supply center for the construction of the highway in 1942. Known as the Alcan Project, it provided an overland route from the lower 48 for the U.S. Army when it was felt that the Japanese were likely to invade Alaska. Little more than a trail of 1522 miles from Dawson Creek, B.C. to Delta Junction, Alaska then on to Fairbanks, the pioneer work was done in an astonishing time of 8 months and a few days, by the U.S. Army Corp of Engineers, most of whom were black. The next year, Canadian contractors improved the road. By that time the perceived threat was over and the machinery was sold to Canada in 1946 for $70,000,000. During the ensuing 40 years, it has been vastly improved. Most of it is paved. Some of the paving is very good, some very bad. Today, Watson Lake is a key center for lumbering in Southern Yukon and northern British Columbia.

This evening I camped a few miles north in the small village of Upper Liard at the Green Valley RV Park. This is a pleasant campground. It is the first time I have tried a privately owned campsite and it seems to work pretty well. It has a shower, car wash, and gas station as well as a grocery store. And it has a golf course. I passed on the golf course, but the Harley sure needed a good cleanup in the car wash, as did I in the shower. I left Chip on his own for whatever he chose to do about his personal hygiene.

Seeing my obvious fatigue, some other bikers came over to help me set up my camp. A couple from Munich, Germany, Karl and Hilda, had come in on a Motoguzzi. They had a good command of English, but I found my German came in handy in our conversation. The years I served in the Army in Germany where I met and married Gundi, for whom German is her first language, proved useful. Carol and Mark from California rode a Harley Hog. I had met them once a few years ago at Sturgis. They had some problems communicating with Karl and Hilda, so I seemed helpful to them in that respect. The last twosome to join our group was from Kodiak. The other couples had never been to Kodiak Island and my visit there had been a while back, so Maryanne and Joe regaled us with stories of their island that held our interest for some hours.

Two thirds of the desolate, windswept, rocky island is the Kodiak Wildlife Reserve, famous for brown bears and bald eagles. Kodiak is home to a multi-million dollar fishing port, one of the top three in the United States.

Joe wrote articles for some wildlife type magazine. His descriptive storytelling ability made his home island come alive for us. We seemed to see emerald grass gleam in heavy dew each morning and dark spruce forests stand cloaked in perpetual fog. Sunset paints the snowy, jagged peaks in vivid splashes of crimson and gold.

Reminders of its history are visible everywhere on Kodiak Island. Ancient artifacts of the Koniag culture can be uncovered next to relics of the Russian era scattered near dilapidated whaling stations or hollow World War II bunkers. 1912's eruption of Mount Novarupta sent volcanic ash that became the topsoil and still layers the town like a room full of dusty furniture. The 1964 earthquake and tidal wave drained salt marshes where spruce tree skeletons now stand sentinel.

Joe told how the Russian explorer, Shelikof, ordered hundreds of Koniag men to be taken into the tundra and speared to death, then founded the settlement of Three Saints Bay, built a school and brought in the Russian Orthodox Church to teach the surviving natives to read and write Russian and be baptized in the Orthodox faith. This reminded me much of the treatment given Natives of both American Continents by European invaders in the name of religion. How we love and respect our fellow man! May the Universal Oversoul forgive us all.

Maryanne and Joe are both Alaska born and revere their native State. I live here by choice and revere it as much. It is past midnight and Chip retired hours ago. I am having some pain, and practice controlled breathing to get to sleep. The Harley odometer reads 57,632. 278 miles today.

7-8-89

Chip and I left Lake Watson around 09.75. It is mostly cloudy, but I am hoping for no more rain as the worst part of the road is ahead. Rain, bad roads and motorcycles don't mix well. I often choose to wait out wet weather when that is a choice. I got lucky today. For the first time in seven trips over the Alaska Highway, I didn't get rained on while riding the dirt road, but had a pretty good shower from Summit Lake to Steamboat in British Columbia and glad that section is paved. Also there was enough lightning to give both myself and Chip some concern. Of course he is like a kid hiding under the bed, tucking into the sleeping bag when things happen that he doesn't want to see. Not my best traveling day.

This part of BC is quite scenic and has been called the Serengeti of the North for its diversity of wildlife. Black bear, grizzly and lynx make these high, rugged mountains of the Northern Rockies their home. Almost entirely of stone, I believe limestone, these peaks have layer on layer of exposed, beautiful stratum sedimentary rock faces several thousand feet high and do indeed appear to have risen from some ancient sea bed. Elk, moose, caribou and bison are abundant but several years ago this area had a very large burn and though it improved the wildlife habitat a great deal, it is unsightly and somehow depressing to pass through, although one can sometimes spot a lovely floral valley of tenacious alpine flowers, bluebells, purple asters and white mountain daisies. Or, near hot springs, clusters of delicate orchids. I don't know what species they are. Florence would know. Stone's Sheep are always near Summit Lake and Muncho Lake. I saw about forty or fifty of these Bighorns, mostly ewes and lambs, along the edge of the road. Many mineral licks along the shoulder where pavement meets soil are where they frequently congregate. Lake Summit is the highest point on the highway, but it is not on the Continental Divide. The road crosses the Divide at another, lower elevation.

Fort Nelson sits at mile 300 of the historic highway. It was founded as a fur-trading post about 200 years ago, but developed as construction on the Alcan (Alaska) proceeded. Today, this northernmost town in British Columbia is a growing community and is the center for service and transportation in this region. The largest gas and oil processing plant in Canada is here, as well as one of BC's wood products plant. There is also some agribusiness. Chip and I will camp here tonight at a KOA campground. I can shower, wash the Harley and get a good meal. I am experiencing more pain, but tomorrow I will get to Dawson Creek where there is a clinic. I think I made a serious misjudgment to forego a cancer treatment before leaving Anchorage. If I had done that, I would have been pain free for the summer.

Odometer is at 57,962. 330 miles today.

7-9-89

We left Fort Nelson about 09.30 after breakfast at the little café. I had a bowl of oatmeal with brown sugar and Chip did Cheerios. Neither of us did milk. It seems to give me gas that works against my gut. I was glad for the extra large windshield on the Harley, because the weather was cloudy with frequent showers until Fort St. John, where it finally cleared up. Around Wonowon, (101) one hundred and one miles from Dawson Creek, farming activity begins and increases throughout the Peace River Country. Dawson Creek is a regular farm town that has grown a great deal in the past 25 years. It is in the Peace River Valley; Canada's most northern important agricultural center. Much of it was settled by immigrants from the Ukraine, raising primarily wheat and cattle. Five grain towers were built in 1930. One of the remaining towers was moved and is the current location of Dawson Creek Art Gallery. This is the beginning of the Alaska Highway, Milepost 0 from Dawson Creek,

Canada to Delta Junction, Alaska.

I found the District Hospital and left Chip safe and secure in a saddlebag, wrapped in his towel. Several days ago we had abandoned the box and just kept his towel. He seemed to know to stay put and cuddled in to sleep away the time. I had the pleural fluid drawn out in the ER and was put on a cot to recover for a few hours. I got a motel room, fed Chip the last of his Wheaties and slept through the night. We have come 1649 miles from home. The Odometer reads 58,249.

Chapter 4

Incident at Spirit Lake

7-10-89

Spirit River is located some 50 miles east of Dawson Creek. Here, too, the country is devoted to farming, mostly wheat, canola grain and cattle. The farms and ranches are neat and well kept. This country is referred to as prairie, but it is man made prairie in that it is forest land partly cleared for farming. About half is still woodland.

I feel well again today. No pain for the time being. We breakfasted in Spirit Lake. The café was full of local farmers and business people. Chip and I were included in the general conversation. Lively and interesting, we discussed local affairs and I responded to questions about my trip. When I got up to leave, an old fellow in coveralls asked for my bill. He wanted to pay my tab so I would remember Spirit Lake as a friendly place. Well, I do remember Spirit Lake and its friendly farmers, but mostly I remember my reception outside the café.

Street parking was at a 45° angle, the Harley sat a few spaces to the right of the café entrance. I put Chip on the buddy seat and noticed a woman wearing a burkha crossing the street toward me. She stopped in the street, watching me. I assumed it was her fascination with seeing a grown man take a chipmunk out of his shirt pocket and set it on his motorcycle. Maybe it was the Harley itself. It's a pretty impressive piece of machinery. Because it has a high wrap windshield and the saddlebags aren't the old leather, tie-on ones, but metal and actually part of the bike, with a clothes trunk attached behind the cushion-backed buddy seat, it looks massive.

Now, as a growing boy, Dad had taught me and my brother that it was the courteous thing to do to tip your hat to a lady if you made eye contact with her. Old fashioned, maybe, but was supposed to convey that the man was no threat. I was wearing my black leather biker's cap, and since there was no way to ignore the woman, obviously Muslim, I tipped my cap to her. She made no move and I wondered how I was going to get around her on the street when I left, but figured she'd walk on by then.

To mount a big tour glide bike, it is easiest for a short fellow like me, to bend my knee and lift my right leg over the bike with my right hand, steadying with my left on the handlebar. This I did, and started the smooth evolution engine that is one of the custom features of the Harley. The woman walked straight up to me, so I looked at her, expecting some question or greeting, but what I got astonished the hell out of me. She spat directly in my face, then turned and walked away.

I served in the Army in Europe for 8 years and visited most countries there; I served 4 years in Japan and Hawaii. But never in the Middle East. I am fairly well acquainted with many cultures and their customs, I speak German, fairly decent Japanese, and am working on Spanish. I have studied religions, including Islam, but not their culture or customs. I was at a total loss for an explanation. Why would she spit in my face? What did I do to her? I turned off the Harley, tucked Chip into a saddlebag, and went to the café restroom to clean my face and jacket. Back at the Harley, someone else was waiting for me. A retired Royal Canadian Mounted Policeman.

He reached to shake my hand. "Got you good, didn't she?

You know why?"

"Not the slightest idea," I was not in a particularly pleasant mood anymore.

"Well, I'll tell you. When you got on your bike, you lifted your heel to her."

"I lifted my heel to her? When was that?"

"When you bent your leg to get on your bike, your boot heel was facing her. That's lifting your heel to her. She's a Muslim, that's an insult. You didn't know, she didn't care that you didn't know."

"Is that some Islamic tradition?"

"Actually, it's in the Christian Bible. Both Old and New Testaments, I believe. But you know why I am here? I am collecting signatures on a protest petition. This town is full of Sikhs and lots of the men want to join the RCMP. But they want to be allowed to wear daggers and turbans as part of their uniform. Well, mister, the RCMP has a uniform that goes back a whole lot of years and it does not include daggers and turbans. If they want to wear our uniform, fine, but it can't be modified to suit their religion. Would you care to sign?"

I hesitated. "I'm not a Canadian."

He shrugged. "Are you American?" I reached for his petition and signed it. I lifted my heel and got on the Harley and rode out of Spirit Lake.

Chapter 5

Canadian Trivia

Dunvegan Provincial Park is an historic settlement on the bank of the Peace River and the site of one of Alberta's early fur trading and missionary centers. The Beaver Indians lived in this area when the first European explorers passed through in the 1700's. In 1805, Archibald MacLeod established a trading post and named it Fort Dunvegan after his family's ancestral castle in Scotland. Dunvegan became a Hudson's Bay Company post until 1918. The Factor's house and St. Charles Catholic Mission Church and Rectory are the only buildings standing from that time, but restoration is being planned on the Anglican Mission, St. Savior. A stone pillar in a grove of Manitoba Maples now marks the site. The maples were planted in 1888 by the Reverend Alfred Gariosh, pastor at St. Savior, to commemorate the death of his daughter Caroline. Her grave stone still stands among "The Maples."

St. Charles was established by Father Emile Grouard in 1867 and he decorated the altar with his own paintings. Nearby is a statue of Our Lady of Peace, erected by the Knights of Columbus, overlooking the Peace River.

Currently The Market Gardens attract visitors to buy the abundant produce raised in the area. The Dunvegan General Store is just that, a general store. Anything from an ice cream cone to a junk souvenir can be purchased there. Strawberries at the Market were tempting but difficult to eat while riding, so at the General Store I bought lunch, a Hershey bar for myself and trail mix for Chip. I wanted to make up as much road as I could.

A ferry was used to cross the Peace River at Dunvegan from 1909 until 1960, when the longest suspension bridge in Alberta was built. I believe it is the only suspension bridge in the Province.

The Peace River flows from the mountains of British Columbia to the Arctic Ocean. It got its name because it was on this river that the Cree and Beaver Indians settled a peace agreement between their tribes.

★★★★

Grimshaw, population about 2400, is located on the highway at mile 0 of the MacKenzie Highway. The town was named after Dr. M.E. Grimshaw, who set up a medical practice in 1914. This area is a railway center for oil, gas, forestry and agriculture. The tourist booth is an old caboose. In 1985 I had followed the MacKenzie Highway as far as Hay River, NWT. It is named for Alexander MacKenzie, an early Canadian explorer. He is prominently commemorated in this area. I picked up a brochure to read while I had a sandwich in a small eatery. It seems he was convinced that Cook's River in present day Alaska, could provide a water route from the Atlantic to the Pacific Oceans; a mythical "Northwest Passage" that would open a gateway to the vast Oriental trading markets. He paddled off in a birch bark canoe and came back a hundred days later from the Arctic Ocean, not the elusive Pacific. In 1793, he tried again, and this time succeeded, but not by water. On a rock near the Pacific, he painted *"Alexander MacKenzie, from Canada, by land, the twenty-second of July, one thousand seven hundred and ninety-three."* His claim to fame preceded Louis and Clarke who arrived at the coast in 1805.

All well and good for Mr. MacKenzie, but I want to get to

Lesser Slave Lake to camp tonight if possible. Luckily, the weather is perfect for riding, the days are very long, and my treatment at Dawson Creek has me feeling pretty well, and I'm taking it easy, seeing some nice country as I go through Canada's 'breadbasket,' so I'd better leave the brochure for the next interested person and be on my way.

★★★★

Lesser Slave Lake is the largest lake in Alberta, located in Big Lake Country and borders the eastern part of Peace Country. The Cree named it Slave Lake, meaning stranger, for those who occupied it before the Cree. Now it is known as Lesser to distinguish it from Greater Slave Lake a few hundred miles north in NWT. The country around here is rangeland, supporting grass and cattle more than farming product. The greatest attraction is the huge lake itself, a Mecca for fishing, camping and hiking on bike and mountain trails including the Trans Canada, and rare old growth forest "Walk Through Time Trail". I have plenty of daylight left to find a good campsite and get some chores done. Luckily, I found space at the Bay Shore Resort edging the lake, more expensive, but with power, showers, restrooms, a store, Laundromat, gas station and several nearby restaurants. I set up my tent and lay down to rest for a while. Chip was restless, but soon calmed down and stayed on the Harley to keep watch. After napping for an hour, I woke to find him on top of me. Crows circled overhead, watching for food scraps and Chip preferred not to be one.

Aside from my experience with Islamic custom in Spirit Lake, I find Canadian people, without exception, to be friendly, open and eager to visit. Here at the camp, about a dozen college kids had three camping spaces next to mine. Bored with fishing, they surrounded me to offer help. A couple of the young men thought the Harley was created by God himself and wanted to wash and service it. I showed them how to clean it properly and they got right to it. I watched for a while, but they seemed competent and did a very good job. I keep the saddle bags locked. I had a small safe installed in one where I keep considerable cash for my trips. A few thousand dollars right now and I have the keys in my pocket. Some of the girls wanted to do my laundry and when I hesitated they grinned and said they wash their brother's clothes all the time, so they know what male underwear looks like. That's not it. I was career Army. I do my own laundry, even at home, but it was a nice gesture. Then Chip and I headed for the grocery to stock up on supplies.

I thought it only fair to ask them to have dinner with me at one of the eating places, but they had other plans, insisting that I have the evening meal with them. As it turned out, they attended the University of Alberta in Edmonton. It seems they were taking a week vacation from summer studies to relax and enjoy the Lake Country. Their accommodations were three large Mercedes RV's. University perks? I wondered. More likely parental perks. They put out quite a spread of food and we sat around the picnic tables talking well into the night. Two of the men and one girl were involved in studies with the National Research Council laboratory in Saskatoon, and another girl, studying to be a research oncologist, worked through the Medical Research Council there as well. There was some discussion about Atomic Energy research studies, the Nuclear Plant at Ottawa and Uranium mining in the area. I volunteered my involvement at the Nuclear Plant in Sundance, Wyoming, and research into Thorium instead of Uranium, since Thorium is a more benign mineral and can be transformed into U233 for nuclear energy, safer than the Uranium U234, and heating iodine for radioactive fuel, which unlike water, will not cause a dangerous environment in case of a spill. The medical student joined in that Thorium and Iodine are used for radiation in certain cancer treatment, so it made sense to her. These young people really were not kids at all, but they were students. This was all theoretical to them. I didn't mention that I carried Meso in my chest. I'm sure the med student never guessed.

At length, I realized the time and said I must retire, since I would be on the road again in the morning. I thanked them for dinner and a stimulating evening and went back to my tent, tucked Chip in for the night, crawled into my sleeping bag and listened to the lapping waves of Lesser Slave Lake until I fell asleep.

I had checked the odometer before dinner. It read 58,552.

Chapter 6

On Little Loon Lake

7-11-89

Not much of note today. Saskatchewan is true prairie, though up to here it is largely wooded except where it has been cleared. It is definitely the result of ice age glaciations. Interesting in a way. I think it could grow on one. I dodged a lot of shower activity and only got caught once. I camped in the rough at Little Loon Lake near Glaslyn. This is a tiny village surrounded by recreational lakes. Its population is about 375 regular residents, but that swells considerably during tourist season. The people are very warm and welcoming. Pride of the town is its eight sided water tower, one of two in Saskatchewan. Impressive. The Little Loon Regional Park is about 5 km east of Glaslyn with a couple of dozen electrical plus water sites, about the same number of non-electrical sites and quite a few overflow sites. All the sites were full except a few in the overflow section. Here camp sites are little more than a board nailed to a tree with a number, and raised fire boxes. I was assigned the last one, far from the Convenience Center, but close to the lake. Chip and I got a bite to eat at the Camp Kitchen, and bought a few supplies at the store. I called Gundi at a pay phone to let her know where I am and see how she is getting along. She works at Safeway and has several friends there, so does not lack for company. Our daughter Karen Elaine has gone to Los Angeles for the summer and our granddaughter Meghan is staying with Gundi. Made me a bit lonesome for home. I decided not to pitch my tent tonight, just sleep under the amazing array of stars; brilliant in the darkness, close enoug to touch.

Mind is a powerful thing. Most of the time I keep my cancer at bay by simply not thinking about it. I believe it was Richard Bach that said if you erase a problem from your thinking, it does not exist for you. But tonight, melancholy seems to have me by the throat and the cry of loons does not help. That sound is something like the cliché of train whistles in the distance. Long and lonely. I lie there, looking at the stars and listening to the loons and a passage of Walt Whitman's "Song of Myself" goes through my mind. *"And as to you Death, and your bitter hug of mortality, it is idle to try to alarm me. To his work without flinching the accoucheur comes, I see the elder-hand pressing receiving supporting, I recline by the sills of the exquisite flexible doors, and mark the outlet, and mark the relief and escape. And as to you Corpse I think you are good manure, but that does not offend me. I smell the white roses sweet-scented and growing, I reach to the leafy lips, I reach to the polished breasts of melons. And as to you Life I reckon you are the leavings of many deaths, No doubt I have died myself ten thousand times before. I hear you there O stars of heaven, O suns, O grass of graves, O perpetual transfers and promotions, If you do not say anything how can I say anything?"*

All my life I have admired stoicism and tried to practice it, but sometimes it does not work. Slow tears come to my eyes and still the loons keep calling.

Chapter 7

Lower Forty-Eight

7-12-89

58,994 miles on the odometer

From Glaslyn Chip and I followed Highway 3 all the way across Saskatchewan to Manitoba. About 50 miles from the Sask/Man border, the weather went from cloudy, showery and cold, to warm and clear. I must have passed through a weather front of some kind. That cheered up both myself and my lively little critter companion. I hope I can keep my new, lucky weather for a few days. Sask is surely the penultimate prairie province and at this latitude anyway, seems to be hay, wheat, lots of lakes and ponds, cattails and Redwing Blackbirds. Being seed and berry eaters, they do not frighten Chip and he puts on bravado to chatter at, or with them. I admit their voice is more cheery than loons. It is indeed interesting country in its own way. The last town in Sask is Hudson Bay, nestled in the Red Deer Valley. A community of around 2000 people, it is a scenic area. I understand it was once an important supply depot for activities on the Hudson Bay. A family style restaurant served up good "country cookin'" and did not object to Chip sharing bread with me. The waitress even brought him a dish of blueberries. Several kids at nearby tables came by to pet him until he had enough and hid in my shirt pocket. I stayed at a small campground at the edge of town.

59,375 miles

7-13-89

After breakfast at the same restaurant, we got on the road again for Manitoba. The name Manitoba is from the native Cree word, *manitowapow* meaning 'strait of the spirit'. The sound of waves and pebbles on the shores of Lake Manitoba was the source of Indian belief that the Manitou of the lake was beating a drum. Who am I to disagree? The province is still home to many Metis Indian tribes and other natives.

The Manitoba border abruptly transitions to woods and less prosperity. Of course as you travel east in Canada, it is obvious that activity is steadily pushing southward until at Winnipeg it pretty much collides with the US border. This too, moves a little south as if to give Canada more room to live in. It seems to me to be very similar to Saskatchewan. I did see more cattle and less wheat, but I'm sure that is largely a matter of where you look. The weather has sure turned out nice for now. Hope it holds.

Considered 'The Gem of the Prairies,' Winnipeg is a city that combines natural beauty with a high level of ethnic diversity, home to over 43 different nationalities. It is the largest city in Manitoba, population over 685,000. I cruised through the main drag where many ethnic cafes line the streets, offering hand made cuisine. I found an Asian sidewalk stand and bought a Kung Pao Beef bowl for lunch. Chip got some rice and peanuts and stuffed his cheeks. It isn't unusual to find his tasty treasures hiding in my saddlebags.

We crossed into the US at Emerson, Man. In 1873, two American business men, Thomas Carney and William Fairbanks, became interested in land on the east side of the Red River at the Canada/US border, with the intent to establish a town at that location. About a hundred settlers arrived that year and in 1874 the settlement was named "Emerson" after Ralph Waldo Emerson, who was Fairbanks' favorite writer. Ten years later, it had a population of more than 10,000. Several elaborate "Italianate" style homes remain from that period. Emerson is called "The Gateway to the West," and Fort Dufferin was established on the west side of the Red River by the North West Mounted Police, (now the Royal Canadian Mounted Police). The major reason was to keep law and order due to the onslaught of settlers, rustlers, and outlaws to the area. It was also the site used by the International Boundary Commission in mapping the border in 1874. Some of the old derelict barns and the Officer's quarters still stand in hayfields.

Following the Red River Valley south for 20 miles, we rode into Hallock, MN in the late afternoon and decided to camp here. The moisture is much better than a year ago when I came through this area. Then, they were really dried out. Now it looks about right. Wheat and barley are the major grains grown, but sugar beets and sunflowers are specialty crops. Hallock is conveniently located for marketing and processing of raw products. Sugar beets are processed at the American Crystal Sugar Company in Drayton, North Dakota some 20 miles southwest of Hallock.

I set up camp at Horseshoe Park. Several Winnebego campers were parked there. Mine was the only tent. Most of the campers were Canadians who come for groceries and gas since it is much cheaper here. Again, I find the Canadians to be friendly, open and ready to visit. Because Horseshoe Park has no showers, we all went swimming at the Municipal pool before finding a place to eat. Chip declined my invitation to join us in the pool, but hastened to have dinner with us.

We have traveled 3167 miles from home Odometer at 59,767 miles

7-14-89

We got on the road at 0800 hours and stopped for breakfast at the only café in Kennedy, (population 165) on US-59. Several farm folks were having morning coffee and conversation. Chip and I were invited to join them and they pushed a couple of tables together to accommodate us. This is so common in these locations, it is almost expected to entertain the stranger in their midst.

Weather is too hot, too cold, too rainy, too dry. Grasshoppers are the biggest in the Mid-west, in the United States, in the world.

"They carry off small mice, rabbits, kids. I seen one seven inches long 'tother day. Flew a good twenty feet. He'd a carried off yer munk there, bet."

"Grasshoppers don't carry meat around, ya dang fool! They're vegetarians. I seen one 'most a foot long. Pulled up a whole corn stalk and flew to Nebraska 'fore it stopped." General guffaws.

Government programs were cussed and discussed. George HW Bush seemed to be on the right track. Might try to reduce farm subsidies some more to save taxes. Well, he couldn't be any worse than that peanut farmer a few years back. Actually, that actor fella from Californ-i-a took a narrow view of subsidies. Good thing Congress held out for us on the land. Course, nobody did as much for the farmers as FDR. Oh, come on. That's ancient history. We mostly agreed that nobody likes government programs except the ones we personally benefit from.

Chip and I rode south on US-59, about as straight a highway as it gets. Lots of wheat. From the amount of wheat I have seen in the last two days, people all over the world must eat a lot of bread. Or Wheaties.

I stopped at the **Super 8** in Appleton (Where the Prairie meets the Water) for the night. Did laundry, washed the Harley and ate in my room. I was pretty tired. These straight highways tend to wear me out with boredom.

Odometer reads 60,060

7-15-89

Still traveling on US-59 South. Montevideo marks the westward limit of the edge of the "Sioux Uprising" in 1862. This was when the local confederation of tribes under Sioux Chief Little Crow rebelled at the continuing breaking of treaties by the government in Washington and attempted to assert their autonomy in the area. This was, of course, promptly quashed after the manner of the time. Montevideo is the site where Little Crow tried to reason with both sides. Was he a traitor or savior to his people? I guess each label could be argued. He tried to lead his people and listen to the whites. He dressed as a white man, built a house near Montevideo and started a farm. But with all his efforts, he got nothing that was promised him by the Buchanan government.

Little Crow was the 4th generation to become Chief of the Sioux Santee band, also known as the Eastern Dakota band. His name before it was changed to Little Crow, was Taoyatiduta, (his people are red) and he signed the treaty of 1851 with that name. He had 6 wives and 22 children, 7 of whom were living at the time of the Massacre. After the uprising, he never wore white man's clothes again. He returned to Minnesota to steal horses for the Plains Indians. Little Crow was killed by bounty hunters for $500 and his scalp hung at the Minnesota Historical Society. In 1971, that relic was returned to his grandson who buried it with the rest of his bones among his own people.

Riding on through Montevideo, we got into the land of soybeans and corn. And more straight roads. I am getting used to them now, nice and comfy in a way, less energy to ride, but still boring. Thunderstorms threatened increasingly until about 4:30 PM, when it began raining in torrents. I put into Harlan, IA for the night. It is located in Southwest Iowa, 11 miles north of Hwy I-80 between Des Moines, IA and Omaha, NE. A typical little farm town with a few motels along the highway and several eating places.

60,344 mi

7-16-89

From Harlan, IA via US-59, Chip and I went to lunch in Shenandoah. Some interesting trivia about Shenandoah, IA. A Nature Trail that starts here is the old Wabash Railroad bed. During the Depression hillbilly singers all had versions of "The Wabash Cannonball." Actually, the song is based on a tall tale about Paul Bunyan's brother constructing a railroad known as the Ireland, Jerusalem, Australian & Southern Michigan Line. The 700 car train he built traveled so fast it arrived at its destination an hour before departure. Finally it took off so fast it rushed into outer space and for all we know is still traveling there. When the train-riding hobos learned of this train, they called her "The Wabash Cannonball" and said every station in America heard her whistle. When the song was popular, the Wabash Railway named its express run train from Detroit to St. Louis, The Wabash Cannonball. I have an old 45 record of Roy Acuff singing it.

"Now the western states are dandies so the southern people say, from Chicago and St. Louis and Peoria by the way, to the lakes of Minnesota where the rippling waters flow, no chances will be taken on the Wabash Cannonball.

"Listen to the jingle, the rumble and the roar, as she glides along the woodland on the hills and by the shore, hear the rush of the mighty engine, hear the lonesome hobo's call, he's aridin' through the jungle on the Wabash Cannonball."

So how about that, Chip? Did I do okay?

At Shenandoah, we took IA-2 east, passing through spot-in-the-road towns along the way. Mt. Ayr, Leon, Corydon, Bloomfield, Ft. Madison, Keokuk, and in Missouri, Canton, Hannibal, Bowling Green, I've been everywhere, man, I've been everywhere. Then we edged into Greater St. Louis and on to the suburb of Woodson Terrace, arriving at my sister, Phyllis's house around sundown. She had been waiting supper, so after making accommodations for Chip, we ate, did the dishes and sat to visit. I was exhausted and took off my boots to lie on the couch. At midnight, I heard the clock chime, found myself covered with a blanket and Chip sleeping in one of my boots. Phyllis has always been a thoughtful person. A bed was prepared, but I turned over and went back to sleep.

Chip and I spent a couple of days with Phyllis. One day we took the Harley and had lunch at the old Union Station. Then Phyllis took me to Sears for a photo shoot. She was right, none of my siblings had recent pictures of me. That did not bother me, but it did bother Phyllis. She works for a medical insurance company and knows all there is to know about most diseases. At this late date, there was no stopping the Meso that was killing me less than softly. If I was going to have pictures made, now was the time to do it. We had dinner at her favorite watering hole, a pasta place. Not exactly low fat diet, but very tasty. The next evening was a special treat. She made a pot of pinto beans and ham with cornbread. High gas eating, but I have had little pain since my suck-out in Dawson and dared it to bother me.

7-19-89

60,830 on the Harley odometer

I headed for Pittsburg, Mo to see another sister, Florence and her husband Dale. She is Phyllis's twin. We followed I-44 to US-50 at Union, then 50 to MO-28 to MO-42 to US-54 to Hermitage. Missouri roads are excellent for motorcycling. It seems to me that of all the places I have ridden, Missouri has the best overall conditions. The roads are well marked, well surfaced and well maintained. The terrain is just the right mix of hills, forests and open country. It is never dull and without the long straight-aways found through so much of the Midwest. There isn't the congestion of roads in the east, and many more byways than in the west. I find pure joy in riding through Missouri and Chip seems to share that. He clung to my shoulder, face forward. We arrived at Florence's and Dale's farm at 4:30. They bought this farm that lies along the shores of Lake Pomme de Terre after Dad passed away in 1970 and Mom moved to Topeka. It is familiar to me from visits here with Gundi while I was still in the Army. I had even bought some property at Windyville, thinking we might live there when I retired from the Army. I drew up plans for an underground house to build there. But when I was stationed in Alaska, I knew that was my final home. I have never been sorry. I sold the Windyville property in 1978.

Florence and Dale built a beautiful new house, a real stunner, but Mom's and Dad's old house still stood near it. I explored it for memories and went through the old horse barn. A familiar horse smell pervades it. That's a good smell. The chicken house roof is falling in, but it is hidden among the sunflowers and tangles of vines.

I parked the Harley in their garage so Chip would have a place to stay and feel safe away from owls, cats, and other natural predators that occupied the farm. In the evening, we sat on the deck with drinks and Dale grilled barbeque spareribs to have with roasting ears and fresh salad from Florence's garden.

While we ate, I told them about my experience with the Muslim woman at Spirit Lake and that the RCMP had explained the insult I was supposed to have committed. "But I still do not have any idea why lifting your heel to a person is an insult."

Dale offered to enlighten me. "Well, it's probably in the Bible because the Israelites wandered in the desert with the Arabs. God gave them manna, but not toilet paper and nobody hauled toilet paper around on their donkey. When they took a dump, they wiped their butt with their heel. More than likely, still do." Florence choked on the sparerib bone she was gnawing and reached for her Scotch-on-the-rocks. I held up the corn cob I had just stripped. "If I remember right, this is the All American way." Dale laughed and forked more salad into his plate. "I think I'll stick with toilet paper."

Florence got up and began clearing the table and said she thought that was enough enlightenment for one day. We helped take food and dishes inside. No matter time of day, indoors or out, Florence set her table with nice china, sterling, stemmed crystal and linen napkins. We kept our conversation in a more orderly direction as she served chocolate pudding cake and vanilla ice cream with Kailua Coffee.

For two days, I walked around the farm with Florence and Chip, ate well, rested and did nothing. On one of our walks, Florence said, "Warren, what will I ever do without you?" "Just be Florence." I told her.

I have, in times past, seen Fox Fire in the woods here at night, but nothing this trip. Fox Fire is the result of swamp gasses igniting and flaring when the earth cools the soggy wood swamps at sundown. Maybe it is too dry this year.

The Harley reads 60,095. I have traveled 4495 miles from Anchorage.

7-22-89

We headed to Goessel, KS via US-54. Thunder showers hit all around me but I didn't get wet. I stopped once, joining several big-rigs at a rest area, to take shelter from lightning. On a motorcycle, it is more fearful to me than in a car. The car acts as a shield, but on a bike I feel very exposed to lightning and usually stop when it is active. Chip isn't crazy about it either. I kept my eye out for tornados as well. This is prime country for spawning twisters. A wide variety of crops are grown in this part of Kansas. Rye, Sorghum, Oats and Barley as well as Soybeans line the highway. It all looks to be in good shape to me. Plenty of moisture. But that is to an untrained eye. The farmers may have a different perspective. At times, too much moisture is the problem. Most of the towns look prosperous and growing, but passing through the old oil fields east of Wichita gave the impression that they are not very active. I didn't see any operating pumps. Probably played out.

Kansas drivers are noticeably faster than Missouri drivers. Most of them seem to be doing around 70 on these two-lane secondary roads. I decided to stay off the interstate. More than likely they do 85 there.

Chip and I stayed with my brother Ralph in Goessel. He administers a hospital and nursing home there for Mennonites. Ralph was stationed near Anchorage when he served at Elmendorf Air Force Base there and knows Alaska pretty well.

7-24-89

From Goessel, I detoured back to Topeka to put flowers on

Mom's and Dad's graves there. I stopped at the florist's shop near Memorial Cemetery and looked at the abundance of roses on display. The woman at the counter asked to help me. I told her I was hoping to find some Peace roses, to put on my mother's grave. They were her favorites. And yellow ones for my father. She had several nice yellow tea roses, but no Peace. "Not usual in a florist shop," she smiled. "But hold on a minute. I have an idea." She picked up the phone and soon Chip and I were on the way to her mother's house and her garden full of roses. Peace, Yellow Fortyniners, just about any garden rose in the book. Short, tubby and white haired, she introduced herself as Gladys and asked my mother's name. "Gladys." I left with all the roses my bike would carry. "No charge," she refused my offer. She wouldn't think of charging. I placed the Peace roses on Mom's grave, not in the urn provided. That would not begin to hold them all. But one I put on her name. "Mary Gladys Garrison." The Fortyniners I laid on Dad's name. "Ralph Rose Garrison."

A maple tree has seeded itself at the head of Dad's grave. As I stood there, a leaf floated down and rested on the yellow roses. Memories came flooding in. All of us siblings gathered at Memorial Hospital where Dad was diagnosed with his advanced brain tumor. It was up to us to decide whether to have it surgically removed, or not. Whether to allow him to live indefinitely in a vegetative state, or let him alone to die in peace. Mom wanted to operate and pray for a miracle. We convinced her to let him go.

Mom worked her fingers to the bone for us kids. Canning what she raised in the gardens she planted and harvested to feed us in hard times. She loved to can things. She was canning beans when she had her heart attack. Good way to go, doing what she loved. I flew down from Anchorage early in 1977 and stayed with her here in Topeka to recover from my heart attack. She left us in July that same year. When we all stood here at the grave, the funeral folks waited until we were all gone to put her in the ground. Sis and I stayed behind and threw dirt on the coffin. It is such an old custom and a time honored last farewell.

I will not pass this way again. *Goodbye, Mom and Dad. In spite of your rigid religion, I believe you have been absorbed into the Universal Oversoul. Irony in there somewhere, isn't there?* I got on the Harley with Chip and left Topeka, Kansas. 59 years ago next week, I was born here. *Goodbye, Topeka.*

Chip and I rode on to Council Grove on the Neosho River. There is a lot of history here. After the Santa Fe Trail opened, Council Grove was the only trading post between Independence, Missouri and Santa Fe, New Mexico and was the rendezvous of westward travelers, freighters and traders who crossed the plains. Long before that, in 1541 Coronado crossed the river at this point. No town, of course. The town itself is named for a meeting in 1825 by a council under an oak tree and a treaty between the Osage Indians and the US Government, giving up the right of way for the Santa Fe Trail. Letters from caravans and pack trains traveling the trail were left here at the base of that tree. A plaque says it was called the Post Office Oak.

Seth Hays built the first house/store at Council Grove. It was a log cabin where he lived with his adopted daughter and freed slave. Later, he built a large supply store and restaurant. The Hays House is still in use and I was tempted to get a meal there. Since arriving in Kansas, I usually get a sandwich at a convenience store or drive-in and go to a park or find an outside table to share with Chip. Kansans have a dim view of little grain eating critters and I think are not particularly welcome inside cafes. I passed on The Hays House.

While Chip and I were touring Central Kansas with Ralph, the Harley quit on us near Hutchinson. Ralph found the

Harley Davidson shop there and they sent out a truck and trailer. We loaded my Harley and took it to Hutch. The problem seemed to be the ignition, and we thought we had it fixed, but not the case. After a few miles it quit again, so back to the Harley shop. I needed to replace the rectifier because of abraded wire. So the ignition thing was really a blessing in disguise, or I'd have been in big trouble with the rectifier shorting out. I spent another few days with Ralph, riding around the area to be sure all was well with the Harley before heading farther west. I'd been pushing myself pretty hard and needed to take it easy and enjoy my brother's company.

7-27-89

The Harley was running slick as a whistle and the odometer read 62,057 as I left Goessel with my little munk and rode to Manhattan near Fort Riley. The Fort was first called Camp Center for its proximity to the geographical center of the US. In 1853 the name was changed to Ft. Riley in honor of General Bennett Riley who had led the first military escort along the Santa Fe Trail. The initial purpose was protection of pioneers and traders moving along the Santa Fe and Oregon-California Trails. Later, it became the site of the Cavalry and Light Artillery School and the Buffalo Soldiers were stationed here. Several of the old native limestone buildings are still standing. I understand the world wide influenza epidemic of 1918 started here.

Manhattan is the site of Kansas State University. This ride is through the Flint Hills of Kansas, probably one of the most pleasant areas in the State. The hills are named for flintlike chert that Indians used to make tools, and many artifacts are still being found in the area quarries. There is a commercial endeavor, The Flint Hills Adventures, that offer two hour interpretive tours and trail rides led by a naturalist who expounds on cowboy culture, Indian traditions, plants and animals. I took the dirt road through the Kanza Prairie Tallgrass Preserve that is managed by KState as their research center. Kings Creek Crossing has a grove of hickory and hackberry trees full of woodpeckers and bluebirds. I saw lots of deer tracks, but no deer. Dominant plants are grasses, of course, but also some Indian Paintbrush and blue Penstemon were flowering.

Back on US-24, we rode westward through typical prairie country, largely devoted to cattle and wheat. Lots of corn also, where pheasant flew up along the highway as we passed. Pretty slow fliers, since we saw plenty of road kill. Chip was not excited by all this, (pheasants are grain eaters and he might have liked to join them) and chose to sleep away the hot afternoon. I'm sure it was well above 90°. As we traveled farther west the land is increasingly dry looking and towns farther between. There is, however, irrigation in the Solomon River Valley, which does modify the above.

Near Osborne, the Geodetic Center of the United States has a bronze road marker, determined by the Army Corps of Engineers and is the datum point for all surveying in North America. It has a cross mark and on the point where the lines cross depends the survey of a sixth of the world's surface. What Greenwich is to the world, a Kansas pasture is to North America. A Historical Marker sign is located in Osborne, and reads "On a ranch 6 miles southeast of this marker a bronze plate marks the most important spot on this continent to surveyors and mapmakers," etc.

The Geographic Center of the United States is 42 miles north of Osborne near Lebanon, adjacent to a pasture overseen by a herd of friendly cows. It is a small patch of grass with a 10 foot stone podium and flagpole flying US and Kansas flags and a plaque informing you that this spot marks the center of the continental United States.

By the time a still sleeping Chip and I got to Stockton where we stopped for a bite to eat, we were in Western Plains Country. Yucca and prickly pear cactus are the dominant plants here. The tall grass has given way to buffalo grass. Hawks convinced my companion to seek shelter in his towel again as soon as we hit the highway. Around Oakley, there seems to be quite a bit of sprinkler irrigation for corn, and that cools the air a little bit. Oakley is not, as rumored, the home of Annie Oakley of marksman fame in Buffalo Bill's Wild West Show. That is in Ohio. This Oakley is named for Elizabeth Oakley Gardner, mother of its founder. Near here is "Mt. Sunflower," the highest point in Kansas. Not even a hill, really, at about 4000 ft high. It is marked by a dead tree, a sunflower sculpture made of railroad spikes and a humorous sign warning of altitude sickness.

I was pretty tired from riding in the hot weather, and decided to get a room at a motel in Oakley for the night. I got a hot meal at a little café, had it put in a 'doggie bag' and took it to the room to share with Chip. He likes cornbread as much as I do.

The Harley was running smoothly in spite of the heat and the odometer registered 62,299. I have experienced some cramping, but for the most part remain pain free.

7-28-89

From Oakley, we took US-40 that more or less parallels the Union Pacific Railway on its way across the high plains. This is the general route of the old Smoky Hill Trail which was used by several stage lines and trading caravans. Fort Wallace was one of the main Army installations along this route with the responsibility of keeping the Indians under control. The Indians, understandably, did not appreciate all the traffic crossing through some of their best hunting grounds and made periodic efforts to curtail it. This is, I guess, as near you can get to the heart of traditional buffalo country. A museum about Fort Wallace is on Highway 40 a few miles from the actual location, though the post cemetery is still in place. Nothing else remains.

Into Colorado, still on the Smoky Hill Trail, we passed through familiar names. Cheyenne Wells, Arapahoe, Kit Carson. A few miles south of here is the site of the notorious Sand Creek Massacre, where Colonel John Chivington and his troops engaged in the wanton slaughter of Cheyenne and Arapahoe women and children while their men were away hunting.

This is truly high plains. Once the homeland of the Sioux, Cheyenne, Kiowa, Comanche, Arapahoe, Blackfoot and other horse riding hunters and warriors this is truly where the buffalo roamed. Spanish horses, half Arabian, half Andalusian were initially brought to the grasslands in 1541 by Coronado. Plains people greeted the horse with something akin to veneration and they soon became expert riders and peerless breeders, using only the best stallions for stud. Eventually they evolved into the Indian pony whose smallness belied its actual speed and responsiveness. The writer and artist of the old west, George Catlin, compared the Comanche, those most excellent of riders, to 'centaurs of Greek Mythology', half man, half horse. To the white man these pintos, duns, and paint cayuses seemed no match for their grain fed mounts, but in battle or on the hunt, these pony's far exceeded the European breeds.

As to the buffalo, they provided food, shelter, clothing and tools for the nomadic tribes. And the horse made hunting them so much easier. Warring among tribes was mostly the art of stealing each others horses. I enjoy riding around in this country so much it seems almost sinful. I don't know what hold it has on me. I guess if I have any roots, this is where they are. Maybe in some past life this was home.

Between Cheyenne Wells and Kit Carson is a monument that

reads: *"The route of the famous Smoky Hill Trail. Emigrant and Stage Road extending from Kansas City (Westport) to Denver, via Ft. Riley, Ft. Hayes and Ft. Wallace. Traveled by gold seekers, soldiers and pioneers, route of Butterfield's Overland Dispatch and Wells Fargo Express. The Trail replaced by the Union Pacific Railroad in 1870."* US-40 generally follows this trail.

We hit CO-94 west to Punkin Center. This is a secondary road, but I like to ride it. Chip thought to see some country, more classic high plains, and clung to my shoulder. Punkin Center is comprised of exactly one house and one cafe and had no problem with a chipmunk sharing my plate. I asked the man who served us about the History of Punkin Center and he sold me a newsprint tabloid that said it all.

Despite the best efforts of writers and editors to spell it the 'proper' way, Colorado's 'Pumpkin Center,' survives as 'Punkin Center' named by Mildred Stevens in 1930. Seems her dad, Sears M. Stevens, built a small store and filling station on four acres at the point where two dirt roads crossed about 29 miles south of Limon in Lincoln County. Now those roads are State highways, 94 and 71. He painted his new store orange, which prompted young Mildred to say it looked just like a big punkin. So when the local papers advertised it as "The Orange Front Filling Station,' it became known as Punkin Center and the name has stuck to this very day. The little paper had a long and detailed account of the many comings and goings of the Stevens family until 1981 and more tales of Punkin Center itself. I put it in my saddle bag for later reading and headed on to Yoder and the road to Calhan.

I spent a couple of hours at the livestock auction barn for old time sake. The El Paso County Fair was on at Calhan, and there will be a rodeo tomorrow. The tiny motel there was full, so I went on to Colorado Springs, which is the County Seat of El Paso County, where motel prices are horrendous, and got a room for $35. I will make my periodic pilgrimage to Elbert in the morning and then back to Calhan for the rodeo at 5:30. There are virtually no camping places on the plains. After tomorrow, I will be in the mountains where I should be able to camp more.

Journal entries made at the motel in Colorado Springs to get caught up. Odometer at 62,472.

7-29-89

Today was a big time nostalgia trip. I rode out to Elbert County at the eastern edge of Colorado's Black Forest. This is not really comparable to the Black Forest in Germany, but is quite beautiful in its way. I stopped by the abandoned one room West Lincoln School where I completed the eighth grade. The door was not locked, so I took Chip and went in. The remembered smells of oiled sawdust swept floors, ink smeared desks, dusty books, settled around me. After 45 years, it was all still there. The old schoolhouse clock, hands broken off, still hung on the wall, on the blackboard were written the names of the last students to attend before the school closed and pupils sent to Elbert. A schoolmate of mine had put them there. My name was among those listed. We were the last.

I went on down the road to my boyhood home and knocked at the door. No one was home. I sat on the Harley and re-lived old memories. The horse barn I helped Dad paint, has been torn down, but the cow barn he built is still there, and the milk cooling house under the windmill. Unbelievably, the mailbox is planted in an old milk can that has Ralph R. Garrison embossed on the side. Behind the house is the bed of wild Bouncing Bettys where Mom played bear one dark night and scared us kids practically out of our underwear. The old root cellar has caved in. The dry wash that raged floods when it rained has been filled in by dozer. The clay bluff where chokecherries grow seems less high. How many late summer days we kids spent there picking chokecherries for Mom to make into jelly. Still the best jelly in the world. She even canned the cherries. They were too small to squeeze the pits out, but good with cream and Mom's homemade bread and butter. We just spit out the pits.

There, near where the old horse barn stood, is the corral where Cheyenne dumped me on my head over and over. I was 12 I think, and had been reading Will James cowboy books. One in particular I liked. "Smokey The Cowhorse." The kid that broke Smokey was named Clint. I thought that was the best name I'd ever heard, and I was saddled with Warren. I asked Dad if I could change my name to Clint. He didn't think that was a good idea, but said if I could ride old Cheyenne, he'd call me Clint. Cheyenne belonged to the Sheriff. Dad trained horses for the Sheriff and other folks. He never broke a horse, he trained them to saddle or harness, depending on the breed. But Cheyenne was a range horse and had been through several hands before and refused to be 'broke.' So Dad was training her to ride and it was not an easy thing. I'd watched Dad train horses before and took on his challenge. That ornery old mare bucked me off plenty of times out of pure-dee cussedness, but finally I gentled her enough to ride her. So Dad called me Clint to the day he died. I have that name engraved on the fender of the Harley. *"Clint"*

I lived here for seven years, from age 10 to age 17, and truly do not know or understand the tremendous hold it has on me. I remember little happiness and much unhappiness in those years, but somehow it seems like home to me. I guess those were my most formative years and put a stamp on me I will never lose. Chip must have felt my sense of loneliness and snuggled into my neck as we rode the Harley on to Kiowa, Elbert County's Seat, to ride past the school where Dad was principal and I went to High School and the Pilgrim Holiness Church we attended. Holy, holy, holy, hallelujah, amen. I managed to bury my bitterness years ago, but though dulled by time, the memory remains.

It was clear, sunny weather and quite warm for me, but not nearly as hot as in the country around Calhan, so I decided to take a break in the Kiowa City Park and picnic lunch with Chip until it was cooler in the afternoon before going to Calhan for the rodeo. Woe is me. I found out that the rodeo was at 1:30 instead of 5:30. Well, maybe tomorrow. I camped at a campground in the Black Forest. Harley said 62,775. Chip said, feed me.

7-30-89

I rode to Castle Rock where Dad bought our first tractor for the Elbert farm. It was in 1945 and farm implements were rationed for the war. It was necessary to put your name in the pool for whatever would become available next. Dad wanted a Farmall-M or a John Deere, but the tractor he got turned out to be a Ford Ferguson. Ralph still has that tractor.

From there, I took the highway to Penrose, where I graduated High School, and on to Florence, then to Westcliffe via Hardscrabble road that has been paved since we lived in Westcliffe. It is still a beautiful mountain drive and inspiring to come over the top and see the Wet Mountain Valley stretching away on both sides. Ahead are the Sangre de Cristo peaks. Crestone, Crestone Needles, Humboldt. I climbed Humboldt one time. Mom was sure I'd get lost, but I didn't. It made for a very long day, though. I didn't stay long in Westcliffe. In the late fall, I hitchhiked to Pueblo and joined the Army. Mom was devastated, but I had to go. There was no way I could go to college unless it was to a Bible College, and that I refused to do. I'm sorry to say that as a consequence, I have no college education.

I rode by "Grand View Ranch" where we lived. The house is

gone now. It was a nicest house we ever lived in as kids. A long, narrow, ugly trailer house has taken its place among the towering Mountain Ash trees and wild flowers in the yard. Tiny Grape Creek still gurgles past. I am sure it is bordered with Dutch Iris in springtime.

A Jane Fonda movie "Comes a Horseman" was filmed in the Wet Mountain Valley about 1978-79. The Grand View Ranch house was bought to be part of the movie set. One gable was demolished, leaving ⅔ that was moved to the North end of the valley near Deweese Dam toward Texas Creek. The pastureland there is more prairie grass, less lush than in the middle of the valley at Grand View Ranch. In the movie, our old house was home to Jane and her hired hand, played by James Caan. The major Cattleman, played by Jason Robards, ended up killing the banker who planned to take over the cattle ranches for oil drilling. Jane found the bloody body hanging upside down in her bedroom closet. That was Ralph's bedroom closet. Actually, I found it a little chilling to recognize the closet when viewing the movie. At the end, the house was burned down as part of the action. Time moves on, but that house was a very nice, if small, part of my past.

I took Texas Creek to Cotopaxi, then back to Florence, CO for the night. I took US-50 from there to CO-160 to Walsh, Colorado. My grandparents had homesteaded there in the 1920's before the town was built. When the railroad went through, the bigwigs offered to name it Garrison, but Grandpa wouldn't hear of it. Stubborn old goat. So it was named Walsh after some railroad mogul. I have two cousins living here, Olive Ackley and Loren Eslick. No one was home at Olive's place. I chose not to see Loren. I hit US-50 again to Kinsley, KS. Chip and I have logged 6594 miles on the Harley Davidson.

Intermission

Warren's journal ends here for his 1989 ride. What route he took back to Anchorage is unknown to me. I know he felt due for another treatment for his pleural cavity drainage and that he probably took the shortest way north. Since his cancer disability from ARCO where he was the Maintenance Supervisor at Prudhoe Bay, he was required to take multiple tests semi-yearly, and these were due to be done. He and Connie spent the coldest of the winter months in Hawaii, and he would have serviced and stored his motorcycles for that period of time. Besides the FLT tour glide, he had several Harley Davidson Sportsters. He wrote me frequent letters and phoned fairly often. We kept in contact. Since babyhood, (I was 15 months younger,) we had been playmates and companions. Until Warren started to school, we were "Buddy-boy" and "Sissy." We kind of knew how the other thought and often shared our views.

Warren began his journal entries again in the summer of 1990, but not in Alaska, though he left from Anchor Point. He does not give odometer miles, but miles traveled from Anchor Point, and does not explain his route to St. Louis. Chip was still on board, having hibernated in Warren's garage through the winter. Chipmunks have a life-span of 7 to 8 years. I pick the journal up in St. Louis, although I think he had stopped at Florence's place first, since he begins recording miles from Springfield, MO. Much of this section of his journal is in present tense, suggesting he kept a running account without jotting notes to fill in later.

Vivian Zanini

Chapter 8

Coast to Coast

From Anchor Point, to St. Louis, 5074 miles.

I took US-50 east from St. Louis, crossing the Mississippi River there. Two years ago I crossed the Mississippi, but at its farthest north bridge where the river leaves Lake Itasca in Minnesota. This part is Mark Twain's River. Indeed quite impressive. In Illinois I am in genuine farm country, black soil and flat as a pancake. The wheat is starting to ripen and corn is 8 or 10 inches high. It looks like a lot of rain came early in the spring and farm activity was late getting started. Which may explain why the corn 'is not as high as an elephant's eye.' I passed a number of dairy farms around Lebanon, Illinois.

I stopped briefly at the Mermaid Inn, where it is recorded that when Charles Dickens traveled to America in 1842 as far as St. Louis, he and his entourage stayed the night here. His wrote of his *"Jaunt to the Looking Glass Prairie and Back,"* referring to his stay at the Mermaid and his walk about Lebanon. In 1843 he wrote *"A Christmas Carol,"* supposedly getting some of his inspiration from his stay in Lebanon. It is performed here every year at the Looking Glass Playhouse.

On past Carlyle, in prehistory home to tribes of mound builder Indians, and on to Salem. The New Madrid (Missouri) Earthquake of 1811 that caused the Mississippi to flow backward and rang church bells as far away as Boston,

MA, sent Captain Samuel Young in search of a more hospitable home. Finding tranquility and abundant game at the site of present day Salem, he made camp and decided to stay. In the 1820's severe drought in northern Illinois brought wagon loads of people south to buy food and grain. This was compared to the biblical story of Israel going to Egypt to purchase grain, and Salem became "The Gateway to Little Egypt."

I stopped to buy a sandwich for myself and pretzels for Chip at a local convenience store and asked the significance of a replica of The Half-Way Tavern I saw advertised on the highway. Seems it had a prominent customer, a young lawyer named Abraham Lincoln. He and other attorneys rode the circuit trying cases in those days.

There is also a legend that as the Tavern was a stagecoach stop, one such stage was held up by Indians. The coach was hauling a gold shipment which the Indians made off with. Supposedly they buried the gold in nearby woods. Naturally, people dug for the treasure, and as in the way of legends, it is still buried in the woods there, and folks still dig.

Salem pays homage to favorite son, William Jennings Bryan, famous orator and well known for the Scope's Trial (The Monkey Trial) vs. Clarence Darwin. This trial was the theme for the movie, "Inherit the Wind." If I recall correctly, Bryan was played by Spencer Tracy.

Olney, IL is the home of the White Squirrels. Not just the local High School White Squirrels. A real albino squirrel colony lives in the city park. Olney Central College has a grant from the Academy of Science to study them and holds a yearly squirrel count. Because Chip rides with me, I chose not go through the park to see them.

I have come 5467 miles from Anchor Point. I find it interesting that people along the way in Illinois are friendlier than those in Kansas and Missouri.

I crossed the Wabash River and into Indiana at Vincennes, birthplace of Red Skelton. Flat land became rolling hills east of the river, with less intensive farming and a fair amount of oil production. I passed a drilling rig at the edge of town. Vincennes calls itself the oldest city in Indiana, previously a French fur trading post. George Rogers Clark and his small army of skillful marksmen took it away from the British in 1779. An impressive memorial to him stands in George Rogers Clark National Historical Park. Quite a lot of the architecture here has a strong French influence.

I rode US-50 from Vincennes to Lawrenceburg, IN, just across the Ohio River from Cincinnati, OH. My Grandmother Young, nee Abbott, was born in the Ohio Valley. There is a family rumor that her mother was part Cherokee Indian, and the Ohio Valley, as well as the Carolinas, was Cherokee territory. That seems to support the rumor.

Lawrenceburg is pretty much wine country. Lots of family owned wineries and vineyards follow the old world wine making traditions, so I'm told. I bought lunch for myself and Chip at one of wineries that had a little gift shop and outdoor café. I don't fear that Chip might wander off at these stops anymore. He seems to be quite domesticated and dependent on me. He may scuttle off to do his business, but he never fails to return when he hears the Harley start up.

It was here in Lawrenceburg that I saw a man carrying a cross over his shoulder as in pictures of Christ. The cross was about 8 feet long and made of rough hewn 4x4. Differing from what Christ carried, this one had the trailing end riding on rubber tire wheels, similar to small bicycle wheels. I wondered if he was fulfilling a vow as his part of a bargain with God. 'You give me a miracle, I will carry a cross' sort of thing. It appears common in many religions to do some sort of penance in return for a special favor. 'If you'll cure my Meso, I'll...' I expect if I really believed it, it would work. I prefer to believe like Cardinal Newman, that the Universe knows what it is doing.

Near Bedford, IN, a tornado had passed yesterday. Obviously this one meant real business. It passed along one side of the highway, then crossed over and ran along the other side with truly massive damage to trees and houses along its path. Most buildings were nothing but stacks of rubble. The wake extended for 10 to 15 miles. This was the first time I have seen such extensive ruin. I sure hope I never find myself caught in anything like that. Temp was in the low 90° range and predicted to stay that way. Not too comfortable for an old Alaskan fellow on a motorcycle. From Anchor Point, 5503 miles.

6-16-90

Southern Ohio along US-50 is rather unremarkable. West Virginia seems not to be doing much. It's pretty hilly country, not much farming or anything else for that matter. Maybe some coal mining and moonshining tucked in the narrow valleys. Things seem to perk up a little in the very small areas of Maryland I rode through. I crossed the Ohio River twice, once at Cincinnati and once at Parkersburg. In Maryland I passed a marker proclaiming that Cumberland was where The National Road began. That intrigued me enough to stop by the tourist information center for a few brochures. I picked up some groceries and set up my tent in a small wooded campground just outside the town. Thunderheads threaten, but no rain yet and both temperature and humidity are above 90. Too hot to ride farther today. Chip and I have logged 5849 miles from Anchor Point.

Cumberland, MD got the official name in 1787, but has been a community of some sort for thousands of years. This is probably because it is at the confluence of Wills Creek and the Potomac River. Artifacts point to a civilization in existence here before the time of Christ. In continuous use by American Indians for centuries, it became the site of a European settlement, and eventually a stop for Conestoga wagon trains in the push westward. Because of its proximity to Washington, D.C. and a pass through the Allegany Mountains known as "The Narrows," in 1806 Congress chose Cumberland as the starting point for the Old National Road. This was the first interstate highway that joined the Smoky Hill Trail at the Missouri River crossing. Thisis now US-40, coast to coast.

6-17-90

Packed up before sunrise to get a head start on the day's heat, though it didn't seem to cool down that much at night. We rode through Pennsylvania on US-220 that pretty much borders the Susquehanna River in the Appalachian Range. From Cumberland to Waverly, New York, the river valley is quite beautiful, forested with such a variety of conifers and deciduous trees it must be spectacular in the fall. Many curious rock formations rimmed the valley, results of faulting and folding in this massive range that covers much of the Eastern United States. I saw several deer along the river, and a few road kill. Some flying squirrels excited Chip, but did not lure him off my shoulder. Even the hawks and golden eagles don't frighten him anymore. Guess he knows the Harley is bigger than they are, and it's easy to scamper into hiding. It seems a little bit cooler, here in the mountains, but not much.

At Waverly, I bought lunch at a roadside vegetable market and Chip and I ate under a sycamore tree. He buried some of his trail mix at the foot of the tree, but hopped on the Harley as soon as I started the motor. Waverly is really just a little village on the New York side of Athens, Pennsylvania, the junction of US-220 and NY-17. I took 17 to Binghamton, NY. Nice wooded hills interspersed with small farms, still on the Susquehanna. The Chenango River joins it at Binghamton. At one point in time, this area was a transportation hub for canals, the Erie, Utica and Chenango, but when the Erie Railroad came through, the canal business went bust. Binghamton is still pretty much an industrial town. The one attraction for me is at Recreation Park, site of a collection of vintage carousels going back to 1857. All were manufactured by Allan Herschell Companies of North Tonawanda, NY and the sound of the old Wurlitzer Organ Calliopes still makes me smile. Rides have always been free. On a whim, I took Chip for a spin on a horse with lions hidden in the saddle blanket.

Fun time over, we rode NY-12 to Norwich. Continued pleasant country and historical homeland of the Iroquois Confederacy of Five Nations; Mohawk, Oneida, Onondaga, Cayuga and Seneca. Again Norwich, like Binghamton, is a manufacturing town, from violins to Pepto-Bismol. But there are decent campgrounds in the surrounding forest and it's been a long day. We have come 6197 miles from Anchor Point and 1480 from Springfield, MO.

6-18-90

From Norwich we took state roads that wound through the Adirondacks. NY-12, 28, 30, and 3 to Plattsburgh, NY. Wish I could have enjoyed it more. The Adirondack Park and Forest Preserve is the largest national park outside of Alaska. But it rained heavily for about 100 miles, and I was glad to get to Plattsburgh and dry out. The town is on the shore of Lake Champlain, very scenic, and has a notable French influence. Its proximity to Quebec entices Canadians to shop and vacation here. It is the home of the Plattsburgh Air Force Base, the primary wing of the Strategic Air Command. The 380th Bombardment, Aerospace and Refueling Wings are all stationed at PAFB. These include B-52 Bombers, air-fueling tankers and FB-111s. The landing strip is long enough to land a space shuttle.

After lunch, we took I-88 and US-2 to St. Johnsbury, Vermont. This is maple sugar country. The town itself is known for its Victorian architecture. Some houses are quite magnificent, often four stories high with turrets and bays and wrap around verandas. They offer a walking tour, and I am traveling to see sights and towns and countryside of my United States of America, but walking is not included more than necessary. There was a time in my past, between tours of duty in Germany and Japan, that I walked from Bolivar Missouri to Montrose Colorado and back. There was a time that I skied cross country in Denali, and that resulted in a heart attack when I was 47 years old. So I don't think I will walk the tour today. Besides I'd have to carry Chip, ha, ha.

St Johnsbury has a "Town Forest," but overnight camping is not allowed and lodging here is a little bit upscale for chipmunks, so I stopped at a maple sugar farm and the old Dutch farmer said he'd be more than happy to let me sleep in his barn. His wife invited me to supper and when I declined because of Chip, she said to bring him on in, and we ate a good home cooked farm meal in the kitchen. For a few dollars, she offered a bedroom for the night and breakfast in the morning. I accepted. When I asked to help clear the table and dry dishes, I was shoed out of the house and the farmer took me on a walking tour of his sugar making facilities. This hospitality amazed me for Vermont, but I guess there are exceptions to all rules. 6249 miles from Anchor Point. 1542 from Springfield.

6-19-90

There is no journal entry for this day, except to record that Warren traveled 243 miles. No explanation, but I think it named it 'Babe.' Together they dug the Grand Canyon when he dragged his ax behind him, and created Mount Hood by piling rocks on top of his campfire to put it out."

Rain let up and my time exploring Bangor and vicinity was pleasant. Chip seemed happy to get out of hiding and join me. The little fellow is a real trooper, and good company. We camped for the night in a rough-it type area where we could build a fire and roasted marshmallows for dessert.

From Anchor Point, 6764 miles.

6-21-90

New Brunswick is similar to Maine. Drivers are like all Canadians, wild and undisciplined. For a self proclaimed non-violent society, they sure drive like fiends. However, again I find Canadians to be friendlier to strangers than anywhere in the United States.

New Brunswick is one of Canada's three Maritime provinces and the only bilingual province (French and English.) The Francophone minority is chiefly of Acadian origin. The province is connected to Nova Scotia by the narrow Isthmus of Chignecto. First Nations People have lived here since before contact with Europeans and are called Mi'kmaq, indicating awareness of their spiritual and collective unity. It roughly translates as "my skin friends."

The Augustine Mound has been part of the Mi'kmaq culture for 2500 to 3000 years. This Archeological National Historic Site is in the reserve of the Metepenagaig Mi'kmaq Nation. Considerable evidence suggests a direct connection with burial mounds in the Ohio Valley. Materials from those mounds are found here, a range of rare artifacts that relate to the Adena culture mound builders suggesting sacred and communal rituals practiced by the Adenas in the eastern United States, but seldom seen in eastern Canada. This site is circular, about 30 meters on a low mound surrounded by a ceremonial area. The mound contains human remains as well as traditional artifacts needed in the afterlife. Two ridges, (baulks) in the form of a cross are centered on the mound and oriented in the cardinal directions: North, South, East, West. Each is approximately 1 meter wide and 10 meters long, rising to a height of 0.5 meter in the center. The Augustine Mound retains significant spiritual and ritual meaning to the Mi'kmaq community.

Nearby Prince Edward Island Province was home to Lucy Maud Montgomery, author of the novels about *Anne of Green Gables*. I recall that Vivian read the whole series and at eleven years old, did some pretty dramatic plagiarism in an attempt to write her own novel.

6-22-90

I finally made it to Schooner Pond Head in Nova Scotia, (Latin for New Scotland) the most Eastern point on the North American Continent that can be reached by road without taking the ferry to Newfoundland. I have come 7140 miles from Anchor Point, the most Western point in North America that can be reached by road. It is colder than a witch's tit and lots of rain. Chip opted to snuggle in a saddlebag out of the weather and my hands felt frozen to the handlebars in spite of heavy gloves, so I decided to forego Newfoundland. I'm sure the weather gods were being fractious with me. Not highly surprising this trip. I'm seeing more rain than usual on my summer travels. Average summer temperature here in Nova Scotia is Fahrenheit 65°, winter average, 26°. June shouldn't be as cold as it is right now.

You can surely see the Scot's influence here. Lots of people have the appearance and style of Scotland. You can hear it a little in their speech and, of course, the names. This is very pretty country and I wish it was a little bit warmer so I could ride around and enjoy it. The landscape is heavily forested and hilly with spruce and balsam, some pine and tamarack. Lots of poplars, maple and birch. Wild life all over the place. I encountered a coyote running across the road in front of me and deer grazing along the sides of the road. Sea birds overhead and Canada Geese in the pastures. Some of the low lying areas are marshes and bogs, maybe why the Scots like it. Rocky cliffs along the ocean are crumbling with erosion.

I did make the decision to travel a few km out of the return route to see Grand Pré Historic site, the memorial to the Acadians and I am too close to ignore it so I made it worth the effort. In Seventh Grade, Dad gave me the assignment to memorize Longfellow's epic poem "Evangeline."

I had hot soup in Hortonville and got a brochure. Acadia is touched on so briefly in history books as to hardly be mentioned at all. The French were the first Europeans to explore the St. Lawrence River and the land that is now New Brunswick and Nova Scotia, was called Acadie. By 1668, dozens of French families settled in the Annapolis Valley. Instead of clearing the forest, they built dikes on lowlands and transformed the marshes into rich farmland. The name Grand Pré means Great Meadow. Because of its geographical location, Acadia became involved in the long struggle between the French and British for possession of North America. In 1621, King James I granted William Alexander all of Acadia. Scotsman Alexander renamed it Nova Scotia.

Time and again Port Royal was conquered by the English and retaken by the French. The Acadians did not take part in the wars, although they were French in language and custom. They chose to live in peace on their farms among the Mi'kmaq Indians. The final struggle for North America began in 1754 with the French and Indian Wars, with the English in control of Acadia. The English feared French priests and missionaries would persuade the Acadians and Indians to enter the war, so in 1755, English authorities made each Acadian swear allegiance to the British crown and all who refused were deported and their farms and villages burned to the ground. This, in many ways, mirrors the Cherokee "Trail of Tears" that took place later in United States History.

6,000 were shipped to colonies along the coast from Massachusetts to South Carolina. Some were driven on foot to Louisiana to live among the French settlers there. Descendants of those are called Cajuns and still speak a sort of French dialect. I was in the Army with a couple of Cajuns. Nice men, but they marched to the beat of their own drummer. Health permitting, my plan for next summer is to ride through the Southeast and Louisiana to see Mom's birthplace in Lake Charles. I had a round of Chelation Therapy early this spring and it seems to have done some good. The tumors have shrunk a little and for now are arrested. The cancer will be back, but at least I feel better this summer's ride than last.

Back to Nova Scotia and Grand Pré where some expelled Acadians later returned. When Longfellow's poem "Evangeline" was published in the US in 1847, the story of Acadian deportation was told to the English speaking world and Grand Pré became popular for American tourists who wanted to visit the birthplace of the heroine. But nothing remained except the dikes and a row of old willow trees.

John Herbin, whose mother was Acadian, purchased the land and petitioned the Nova Scotia legislature to grant it Site of Historic Ground for preservation. Herbin built a stone cross on the site of the church cemetery, using scattered stones from the original foundations. In 1920, the Dominion Atlantic Railroad erected the statue of Evangeline and the memorial church. The interior was finished in 1930 for the 175th anniversary of the deportation. All this I gleaned from the literature I found at the church/museum there.

I still remember bits and pieces of the poem. It is about Evangeline spending her life looking for her lover when they had been separated in le Grand Dérangement.

"Sometimes she spake with those who had seen her beloved and known him, But it was long ago in some far-off place, or forgotten......Fair was she and young when in hope began the long journey; Faded was she and old when in disappointment it ended." Finally she became a nun in Philadelphia and in an almshouse found her lover dying. *"Vainly he strove to rise and Evangeline, kneeling beside him, Kissed his dying lips and laid his head on her bosom."*

So much for Grand Pré, Nova Scotia.

6-23-90

Basically, I rode the day backtracking toward Bangor, ME. I stayed the night in Moncton, (pronounced mekten) NB. The city is located along the north bank of the Petitcodiac River at a point where the river bends acutely from west-east to north-south flow. Petitcodiac is the Mi'kmaq tribe's term for 'bends like a bow." Like Turnagain Arm in Alaska, this river exhibits one of North America's few tidal bores. Bores are waves that travel up river on the leading edge of an incoming tide. This tide is from the Bay of Fundy and originally was as high as 6 ft, traveling at 8 mph. Since a causeway was built in 1960, the channel silted in and reduced the bore to about 8 inches in height. It surely does not produce the roar that happens with a bore of several feet like the one at Turnagain Arm.

French Acadians first settled here in the 1670's, established a marshland farming community and named it *Le Coude*. (The Elbow.) Pennsylvania Deutsch resettled after the Acadians were expelled. Presently it is the hub of the Canadian

National Railway System, and eastern terminal of the massive National Transcontinental Railway. Moncton definitely has the look, feel and smell of an industrial city. Rain and cold prevent camping, though there are several campgrounds not far away. As usual in such situations, I bought food at a grocery and ate with Chip in our motel room.

6-24-90

Today I backtracked from Moncton to Calais, ME. I persist in my impression that Canadians are generally friendlier to strangers than are United States Americans. Weather is hard to ride in, cold and rainy with fog along the coast, particularly after St. John. From Calais, took ME-9 to Bangor. This is a back road reminiscent of Alaska, with birch and black spruce. The exception: lots of remnants of past farms with nothing left but piled up rock and former fences. Obviously hard and probably unrewarding labor conditions for extended periods of time. There seems to be little activity now. To keep boredom at arm's length, I started talking to Chip.

"Little Pilgrim, a story told around where Massachusetts joins Vermont and New Hampshire, is by a fellow named Benét. Story called **"THE DEVIL AND DANIEL WEBSTER."** It goes something like this.

'Daniel Webster was a lawyer like no other. He never got to be president, though he wanted to be, but he was the best man around next to God. When he stood up to speak, the stars and stripes appeared in the sky and when he walked along the lake shore with his fishing pole, fish jumped out of the water and into his creel. He could make the harps of heaven play and shake hell to the core. All the chickens he raised were purely white meat, and his big ram, (named Goliath, by the way, Chip) had horns that curled like a morning glory. The biggest case he ever argued was not in any book, for it was against the devil. Happened this way. A man named Jabez Stone lived in New Hampshire at Cross Corners. He was the unluckiest man alive. Not bad, just unlucky. He had a good wife and kids, but never had enough to feed them. If stones cropped up in his neighbor's field, boulders popped up in Jabez's. If his horse got spavins, he'd trade it for one with staggers. But one day, Jabez had enough of the whole rotten thing. That morning, when he was plowing, he broke his plowshare on a rock that hadn't been there the day before. He stood looking at that rock and the off horse started coughing in a way that said horse doctor. Two kids had just come down with measles and he had a whitlow on his thumb. Don't ask me what a whitlow is, Little Pilgrim, because I don't know. But it is in the story. Anyway, Jabez said, *"I vow it's enough to make a man want to sell his soul to the devil. And for two cents I'd do it."*

"Well, story goes, next day Mr. Scratch showed up and took the offer. It worked, too, for seven years, and three years more. Then the mortgage fell due and Stone called in Daniel Webster to argue his case with the devil. Daniel agreed, because if he won, he might get to be president.

"So Chip, do you think Jabez Stone's farm might be hereabouts?" I swear, the little critter had crawled into my jacket and was sound asleep. Oh well, on to Wesley.

At Wesley, (named for John Wesley, founder of Methodism) Chip and I lunched at a little café in an old building. It was serve yourself with several varieties of fish and chowder and other food typical of the region. Not bad, really. Two gas pumps outside with an old sign, "Out of Gas." It is much warmer here than on the coast. I took I-85 out of town to Auburn, ME.

Chapter 9

Westward Ho!

6-25-90

I'm sure Auburn has much to offer, pretty scenery, but I don't much care for New England. I like it better once I get well into Pennsylvania. So I decided to just follow the Interstate until I get out of the East. The Interstate is surely the fast way to go. In some ways easier driving, but much less variety and almost no contact with anything. Fellow travelers seem less friendly and courteous. Just intent on getting somewhere. I did 522 miles today. Camped in a KOA Campground.

6-26-90

Passing through Western Pennsylvania wasn't so bad. I might learn to like it, but am glad to be back in Ohio, crossing the river at Wheeling, West Virginia. On I-70 now, I stopped near Zanesville, OH at the National Road Museum on old US-40.

Zanesville itself has some interesting features and history. It is named after Ebenezer Zane who settled here in 1797 at the point where Zane's Trace met the Muskingum River. Novelist Zane Grey was a descendant of the Zane family and was born here. I read many of his Western novels as a boy. The Roseville Pottery Company exploits the area's clay deposits. I must say it is beautiful pottery. I had a vase sent to Gundi. Probably the most notable feature of the town is its Y-Bridge that spans the confluence of the Licking and Muskingum rivers. It is the only bridge of that type in the United States where one can cross and stay on the same side of the river. "Drive to the middle of the bridge and turn right." Scuttlebutt has it that this bridge has been an aviation landmark for many years. Supposedly, Amelia Earhart said Zanesville was the easiest city to recognize from the air because of the Y-Bridge. Makes sense. One also exists in China, so they say.

6-27-90

My main purpose in coming to Adams County Ohio this trip is to see the Serpent Mound, purported to have been built by the same Adena Culture, as the Augustine Mound I had visited in New Brunswick. I have wanted to see it since I was in Fifth Grade and read about it in the Compton's Encyclopedia at school, but now I was more curious than ever.

Serpent Mound extends about 1370 feet and varies from less than a foot to more than three feet in height. With its head nearing a cliff, it winds back and forth for about seven hundred feet and ends in a triple coiled tail. The head has an open mouth around a 120-foot-long hollow space that holds what appears to be an egg, or the sun. Historically, researchers attribute the mound to the Adena Culture circa 800 BC. There are Adena grave mounds nearby, dating back 2500 years or more, but Serpent Mound contains no artifacts or human remains and was not built for burial purposes. The Cherokee tell a legend of *Uktena,* a large serpent with supernatural power and appearance. The oval head area is aligned to the summer solstice sunset and there has been much speculation as to the significance of this or other patterns, some of which are the appearance of Halley's Comet, light from the Crab Nebula supernova, or the constellation Draco. However, the mound is located on a unique crypto explosion structure that has folded and faulted bedrock which is usually produced either by meteorite or volcanic explosion. What formed the Serpent Mound Crypto Explosion Structure is still debated by geologists. With my knowledge of geology, I tend to agree with those who suggest an explosive eruption of gases derived from a deep magma source; this being one of the few places in North America this occurrence is seen. To my thinking, if such a rupture happened along a curving fault the gases would have flamed on reaching atmospheric oxygen in such a curve, giving the Adena the compelling evidence that a fiery *Uktena* had swallowed the sun. At least that's my take on it. Serpent Mound is a Department of the Interior National Historic Landmark, but I believe is part of the Smithsonian as well.

Chip and I rode to the village of Peebles a few miles to the South of Serpent Mound. We bought some provisions and got a tent camping spot at the Mineral Springs Lake Campground there. Our campsite is right on the lake shoreline, the water so clear you can watch fish swimming by. Very wooded, cool and pleasant as is most of the Ohio River Valley country. I think I may rent a cabin, stay here a few days and do some day trips.

6-28-90

Rented a furnished cabin and took the day off to do some chores. The Harley needed some maintenance and a good wash and wax job, I had laundry to take care of and then an afternoon nap sounded nice for a change. I unloaded some gear to leave in the cabin for a few days. A honeymoon couple had the cabin on one side and when I woke from my nap, a family was moving into the big one of the other side. Of course, the honeymooners kept to themselves, but the family had a couple of kids, a girl toddler and a boy of about

12 who found the Harley more than he could stand just to look at. So his dad brought him over and introduced himself and his son. Dave and Jeremy Nicholson. What could I do but offer the kid a ride? I fastened him in the buddy seat and rode around the lake with Chip perched on my shoulder, since Jeremy had taken his buddy seat. He politely thanked me for the ride and asked if I would like to see his pet. Sure, why not? Well, it turned out to be a Macaw on a leash. Nasty tempered bird that like nipping at one's ankles. Anyone's ankles. Mac and Chip had a few relatively adversarial arguments over the next couple of days when I teamed up with the Nicholson's to do the Kentucky Lincoln Heritage Trail. Jeremy preferred the Harley to his family's sedan and for a kid he was good company. Quite intelligent and had interesting questions about my travels. His favorite word was 'neat,' and he used it often. I was glad his folks trusted me with him.

We caravanned along the Lincoln Heritage Trail, stopping in the National Historical Park to see Lincoln's birthplace at Sinking Spring Farm and his boyhood home at Knob Hill Creek Farm. In 1860 he wrote that his earliest recollections were of this place. We did the Lincoln Museum, and side tripped to tour Mary Todd's house in Lexington. Altogether a pleasant experience.

7-1-90

Packed up my gear and headed back into Bluegrass Country, Lexington claiming to be the "Horse Capitol of the World." Rode past Calumet Farms, Keeneland Race Course and Man O' War's gravesite. Shelby County is home to the American Saddlebred, the only breed of horse originating in Kentucky. During the State Fair in Louisville, some of the Saddlebred farms are open for tours. It was just as nice for me to ride by and watch them grazing in the pastures along the road. Truly beautiful horses.

Considered going down to Mammoth Cave, but decided against it, since I want to make it to Torrance, California to see Vivian this trip. I brought Gundi through here several years ago when we were stationed in Alexandria, Virginia. So I guess I'll forego the fearsome albino crickets in the cave this time and head West. Took back roads through Northern Arkansas and Southern Missouri. Poplar Bluff, West Plains, (where the folks lived at one time,) Branson, Harrison, Neosho, Joplin, Carthage to KC. Plenty of campgrounds along the way and beautiful country, but pretty hot and humid right now. At least no rain.

7-5-90

Have put 69,984 miles on the Harley.

Stayed the night near Edgerton, KS where my father was school principal in the early 60's. Found the location where my parents lived while there.

Chapter 10

Highlights from the Oregon/ California Trail

The trail started in Westport, MO which is now Kansas City. I did not retrace the trail in KC, but picked it up at Lone Elm Campground. Originally known as Elm Grove, because of a grove of trees, travelers cut down the elms for firewood except for one, thus the name Lone Elm. This location is one day's travel out of Westport, where travelers usually stopped to make the organization of the wagon trains and final preparation for the trail. There is a marker in the southeast corner of the intersection identifying this as the Santa Fe Trail. Lone Elm Campground is southeast of the intersection. Take US-56 and a couple of miles southwest of Gardner, there is a marker describing the point where the Santa Fe Trail separates from the Oregon/California Trail after following the same route from Independence, MO.

About 3 miles southeast of Lawrence is a butte called Blue Mound. In 1854, a post office was opened at the junction of two branches of the Missouri Pacific Railroad near the present town of Blue Mound. The postmaster, John Quincy Adams, (yes, that one) was the first settler there and named the elevation Blue Mound, because from a distance it looked blue. It has nothing to do with Indian burial mounds found throughout the mid-west, but was a noted scenic attraction and many wagon trains stopped here to climb the mound for a view. It is the larger and more prominent of two hills, sometimes called Wakarusa Buttes. Presently, the campground there is the site of an annual Music Festival similar to Woodstock.

From Lawrence the trail is closely associated with US-40 to Topeka. Where Douglas County Road 623 runs north from US-40, a marker describes Coon Point Campground, three miles north along DC-623 to the Western edge of the town of LeCompton. In Topeka, take US-75 north across the Kansas River. Just to the east of the bridge is where Pepin Bros had their ferry. From 1842, this ferry took most trains across the river. Now the trail is closely associated with US-24. Following US-24 west, you intersect the trail several times.

Now the trains have been on the trail for about eight days and many of them would reorganize after crossing the Kansas River. Up to then it had been considered essentially a shakedown period. A number of wagons, realizing the hardships ahead, always turned back.

Follow US-40 to Wamego, the trail is in proximity to the highway and sometimes congruent with it. At Wamego, take KS-99 north to Frankfort. This generally goes near or on the trail.

Here I took a side trip to Wheaton, KS where my parents were living when my father died in 1970. Chip and I stopped in a little café and quite coincidentally, the manager was a young man who was in the elementary school where Dad was principal. It was rather an emotional experience for us both. He asked me to stay the night with him and his wife, who had also been a student at that time. I accepted.

7-6-90

The Harley odometer reads 70,220 miles

At Frankfort take KS-9 west to US-77 north for about 7

miles, turn west (left) on a gravel road. Follow this for 1 mile. At a T intersection, turn south (left) and follow for 3 miles. On the left is a steel gate that is locked. Access is on foot via turn-style to Alcove Spring, named by appreciative emigrants who were impressed with its natural beauty and carved their names on surrounding rocks and trees. It is indeed a pleasant place, described in a leaflet of its place in history as *"a beautiful cascade of water, altogether one of the most romantic places I ever saw."* Actually it is not a cascade, but a straight fall of water from a 10-12 foot dirt bluff that interrupts a small creek running from the spring.

This country was a well traveled route of traders and 'mountain men' and in 1842, John C. Fremont and his expedition of explorers bivouacked at the spring. His Donner party, most of whom froze or starved in the Sierra Mountains of California, buried its first member, Sarah Keyes, James's F. Reed's mother-in-law, near the spring. Her tombstone reads, *"God in His love and charity called in this beautiful valley a pioneer mother."* Marcus Whitman's train of Conestoga wagons, with a thousand emigrants to Oregon, stopped here in 1843 to rest and water their stock. Utah bound Mormons and California bound gold-seekers spent time here. Sadly, vandals have done their dirty work on the area, but it is still well worth seeing. I thought once that Chip had left me to stay in this small, secluded valley, but when I took cheese and crackers out of the saddlebag for lunch, he was right there. Not to worry. My little critter has learned where his next meal is coming from.

Near here was the crossing of the Blue River, usually a major event along the trail. The river has since changed course and there are no longer any identifiable features at the crossing. Many crossed the Blue River by ferry at Marysville. I rode there to take a look.

Historic Trails Park is near the site of the early river crossing and has a replica of a rope ferry used at that time. Several trails converged at this ferry crossing, not only the Oregon/California Trail but the Mormon Trail, the Overland Stage Route, The Pony Express Route and the Military Road. At times hundreds of wagon with thousands of pioneers camped in this area awaiting their turn to cross. Charge was $5.00 per wagon and 25¢ per head for livestock. Deaths were common on the trails and many graves are recorded here. Later the Otoe Indians use the Otoe-Missouri Trail when they were forced to move from this area to Oklahoma. Another disgraceful move by the US Government.

I took the opportunity to see the Pony Express Station in Marysville. Although it lasted only 18 months, the Pony Express history has strong appeal in its legend and legacy. Between April 1860 and October 1861, riders traveled day and night through all weather to carry letters from St. Joseph, MO to Sacramento, CA. The one way trip usually took 10 days. Riders changed horses every 12 to 15 miles and rode about a hundred miles before handing off to a fresh rider at one of the 40 or so "home stations." Home Station #1 was at Marysville, a stone barn built in 1859 and leased to the Pony Express in 1860. The barn is still standing and now a museum with quite a bit of historical display. It is well worth seeing. Riders slept at the Barrett Hotel, now the AR-EX Drug Store.

The first rider was Johnny Fry, (historians differ as to the true identity,) who left St. Joe early in the evening of April 3, 1860, arriving in Marysville the next morning. Mail was carried in a special leather saddle cover called a mochila, which fit over the saddle and could not be removed unless the rider dismounted. The four mail pockets, called cantinas, were always locked during the ride. Two minutes were allowed to change saddle covers and mount to ride on to the next exchange. Every rider carried a Bible. Mail was pretty expensive. The original charge was $5.00 per ounce and 5¢ for each additional ounce. Later the charge was changed to $1.00 an ounce + 5¢. Must have been the last time postage went down, not up.

When the telegraph was completed cross-continent, the Pony Express ended, but in June of each year, The National Pony Express Association sponsors a Pony Express Re-ride between Sacramento and St Joseph. Over 550 riders and horses are posted along the way to carry mail. To use a Jeremy word, "Neat."

7-7-90

From Marysville, the Oregon/California Trail angles northwest to the Platte River just east of Fort Kearny, Nebraska. The State of Nebraska has reconstructed some of the old Fort at the Fort Kearny State Historical Park. It is worth the visit. Archeological exploration has located the building sites that are marked with interpretive signs. An interpretive center houses a museum and presents audio-video programs. Replicas of the palisade and blacksmith shop are on the grounds along with some old Conestoga wagons. The various trails converged at Fort Kearny on what was known for a time as the Platte River Road. This was the first Military Installation they passed on the trail. In June, **1849, Lieutenant Woodbury**, stationed at the Fort, wrote, *"Four thousand, four hundred wagons have passed through this post, nearly all destined for California."* In 1850, stage coach service began to run between Independence, Missouri and Salt Lake City, Utah, providing Fort Kearny with monthly mail and passenger service and emigrants used it to send mail back to family left behind, or ahead to family waiting. In 1860-61, the Trading Post was a stop on the Pony Express route.

From Fort Kearny, emigrants were "Off to see the Elephant." The prairies have ended and the Great Plains have begun. A number of places are marked where existing state and county roads intercept the trail on this stretch between Fort Kearny and Ogallala, NE. I camped right on the trail on the south side of the Platte River near Gothenburg. That was something of a thrilling experience and I tried to impress Chip with that exciting news while we ate VanCamp's Pork and Beans under the tall cottonwoods. I hope he appreciated the fact. He seemed more interested in his plate of beans, but who knows what chipmunks think.

7-8-90

Odometer, 70,640

Gothenburg is a nice, small river town with some history to explore. At the convenience store where I picked up some breakfast for myself and Chip, I was directed to the Pony Express Station in Ehmen Park for brochures to local sites of interest. Good way to kill two birds, so to speak. A place to eat and see what else is up.

Of the few Pony Express Stations remaining in existence, two are in Gothenburg. This one was moved from the Upper 96 Ranch where it was originally used as a stage stop and Express Station. In 1931, Mrs. C. A. Williams donated this building to the Gothenburg American Legion, who dismantled it and rebuilt it in Ehmen Park. The second station still stands on the Lower 96 Ranch, four miles south of the town. As part of a privately owned ranch, it is open to visitors on a limited basis.

Swedish Crosses Cemetery is a Dawson County historic site. I found it somewhat reminiscent of the Spirit Houses at the Russian Orthodox Church in Palmer, AK. These unusual and artistic grave markers, made of Swedish steel, were designed and crafted by Benjamin Palm, Gothenburg's first blacksmith, for three of his infant grandchildren's graves more than a hundred years ago. Reportedly, he sent to Sweden for the steel to fashion the crosses that have elaborate scrollwork, stars and hearts that carry Swedish inscriptions of the names and dates of the babies birth and death. The site is on a knoll called "Forever Sweden." How they died is unknown. Was there an epidemic of some disease in the 1880's? Several neighboring children, caught in a prairie fire, are buried here without markers. Can whispered stories be heard here on quiet nights? Or is that creative brochure writing?

The Sod House Museum was established in Gothenburg a couple of years ago. It is a full-scale replica of an authentic sod house used extensively by early settlers in the Central Plains region. The area also features a barn, windmills, and a plow.

I recall stories my father told of when my Garrison grandparents moved from Missouri to Western Kansas to homestead. Grandma and Dad dug squares of pasture and built a sod house while Grandpa plowed the land for crops. What a disaster for land that should have been kept for grazing. It was, of course, the precursor to the dustbowl. Good resource reading for this part of the country is James Michener's Centennial and the Dust Bowl, by R. Douglas Hurt.

From Gothenburg to Ogallala the Oregon/California Trail follows the floodplain of the Platte River to where it forks north and south near the town of North Platte, NE. From there, the trail runs to the south of the South Platte River to ford near Brule. Michener refers to the South Platte River as a non-river that disappears underground from time to time as it meanders across the plains. From the ford, the Trail heads northwest to Ash Hollow.

I took a side trip south to Stratton, NE where my parents lived in 1929 before I was born. This was where they experienced some traumatic events between them which I am sure had a profound effect on the entire family for many years. My father had taken a degree in Theology at the Nazarene College in

Pasadena, CA, and pastoring the Pilgrim Holiness Church at Stratton was his first assignment. He had never really wanted to be a preacher. It was to please Grandma Garrison that he even tried. And failed miserably. Mom anticipated being a preacher's wife when they married and was put out at him big time, resulting in her taking over the preaching duties. That not only humbled his ego I am sure, but did some damage to their relationship. Mom not only loved to preach from the pulpit, it could just as well be a target across the table. Often that was Dad. At any rate, as soon as they could, Dad enrolled in college in Edmund, Oklahoma for his teaching degree. Mom went to live with her parents in Topeka where I was born in 1930. Then she went to live with Dad in Oklahoma where he took his first teaching job at Darlington, OK and in 1931, Vivian was born there. Why did I ride to Stratton? I have no idea, except to see places of our family history.

At Ash Hollow was fresh, clean water – a luxury the emigrants had not tasted since leaving the South Platte River. The groves of ash trees growing in the canyon were a welcome sight after the stark plains. Most wagon trains would rest here for a day or two. Some various postings here are comments left by pioneers. **E.B. Farnham:** *"This is the best looking place we have seen for some time. It is a cool shady looking place fragrant with different kinds of flowers of which rose and jasmine are the principle. Grape vines and currant bushes are plenteous."* **Captain Howard Stansbury:** *"Several springs of delightfully cold and refreshing water are found, altogether the best we have met with since leaving Missouri."*

Ash Hollow has an interesting geological history. The strata known as Ash Hollow Formation, is a prime example of Pliocene history just prior to the last Ice Age. One can see bits of geology, paleontology and some 6000 years old history of early man. Added to that is the distinct mark left by vast encampments of prairie schooners crowding this oasis during the westward migration along the Oregon/California Trail.

These trains entered Ash Hollow from the south, down Windlass Hill. No windlass was used, but the descent was accomplished in several ways. Some tied ropes to the back of their wagons and used man-woman-child power pulling back on the ropes to slow their wagon down. Others used their oxen and still others locked their wheels to make them slide. Freighters usually took loaded wagons down without serious problems. Many emigrants suffered accidents. You can still see deep ruts, almost gullies, dug by the heavily-loaded wagons as they slid down Windlass Hill.

The reward was a pleasant place to camp and fresh spring water to drink. It was also the opportunity to bathe and wash their clothing. Men repaired harness and wagons, animals grazed in the lush grasses. An abandoned trapper's cabin became a sort of unofficial post office and pioneers left letters for relatives 'back east' in hopes that east-bound travelers would take them on their way.

In the valley is one of the few marked graves along the trail. Rachel Pattison died here of cholera. She was 18 years old, married shortly before leaving Illinois and traveling with the family of her new husband. Most of the graves are unmarked because travelers buried their dead in the trail and drove the wagons over them, believing that was necessary to keep them from being dug up by animals or outlaw grave robbers looking for loot.

The Trail reaches the North Platte River near Lewellen, then proceeds along the south side of the river to Bridgeport. A number of trains chose a shorter, but much more difficult route to Bridgeport. Not crossing the Platte at Brule, but continuing on to what is now Sidney, NE, they crossed the South Platte there. A truly brutal trail, but enough shorter to make it worthwhile to smaller trains.

Ash Hollow is now part of the Nebraska State Park System and has numerous cabins and camping sites in this 1000 acre

Park. Chip and I chose to stay here the night, setting up my tent near a small lake. Odometer, 70,824 miles.

7-9-90

I cooked our breakfast on a grill near our tent after I scrubbed it down with sand. Amazingly, my tiny friend has developed a taste for bacon. That is quite a reach for a grain/nut eater. I have to assume it is for the salt, though I give him plenty in other foods. Maybe he sees me eat bacon and since we share a lot of food, has acquired a taste for it.

I gassed up in nearby Oshkosh and we hit the trail again. Follow US-25 west to Broadwater, turn left (west) on NE-92 and follow it to Bridgeport, NE. Then left (south) on NE-88 for about 4 miles. Turn right on a gravel road and you are at the base of Courthouse Rock and Jail Rock. To emigrants who had never seen a mountain, or even a decent bluff, these clay-stone formations were quite stunning. Many pioneers were so awed by these strange geologic features they took the side trip of 4 miles to get a closer look and leave their brand of graffiti, carving names and dates on the sides and summit. Such soft rock erodes quickly and those carvings have long since eroded away. Courthouse Rock can easily be climbed by use of toeholds carved into it by Indian tribes long ago. Such height gave them good lookout posts for game and/or enemies.

From emigrant **David Jackson Staples**: *"We made our noon halt opposite Courthouse Rock bluff; after noon several of our party went over to take a look at it. I climbed to the top and engraved my name and such a view man seldom sees."*

From emigrant **Walter Pigman:** *"We spent about an hour on the summit writing. Our heads became dizzy, we began to hunt the base and had a hard time to overtake our wagons. Being nearly 15 miles off, we traveled hard but did not* *overtake them. We had left camp without pistol or knife, which we ought to have had as wolves and bears became unusually thick."* One has to assume Mr. Pigman's tale ended back with his wagon or we would have no record of his adventure.

A more impressive formation lies ahead for the trail travelers, still in the North Platte River Valley. Follow US-26/NE-92 for 14 miles west of Bridgeport. There these roads junction and immediately off NE-92 is a gravel road leading south. This is Chimney Rock Road. Follow it to the base of Chimney Rock, known as the most famous landmark on the Oregon/California Trail. It has been remarked by earlier residents of the area as well. According to early fur traders, Indians named the unique rock formation "Elk Penis" after the appendage of the adult male elk. (Who'd have thunk it!) This made more sense to those who lived on the plains for centuries, than comparing it to a white man's anatomy. Prim and proper Anglo-Americans preferred the more delicate "Chimney Rock."

So, how tall is Chimney Rock? Using scientific equipment, the US Geological Survey calculated the elevation at 4225 feet above sea level. That was in 1895. Forty-niner David Cosad used the centuries old method of measuring his shadow against the rock to come up with 360 feet from base to top. Today's scientific estimate is 325 feet from base to top. It is believed to have crumbled away some 35 feet in the past century.

How long will Chimney Rock last if it has crumbled 35 feet in a century? Erosion created it, erosion will destroy it. No one cares to guess the amount of time. In 1849, newspaper reporter **Howard Stansbury** said, *"It is the opinion of Mr. Jim Bridger that it was reduced to its present height by lightning, or some other sudden catastrophe, as he found it broken on his return from one of his trips to St. Louis, though he passed it uninjured on his way down."*

This is the same mountain man Jim Bridger who told of petrified birds singing in petrified trees in Yellowstone. Chip took this information with a degree of skepticism.

At Scottsbluff, NE the National Monument is worth a visit. In 1828, a fur trapper, Hiram Scott was wounded and deserted by his companions. By sheer act of will, he made his way to this formation of bluffs along the North Platte River before dying from his wounds. It was for Hiram Scott that Scottsbluff, the county, and the monument are named. Summit Road is the oldest existing concrete road in Nebraska, reaching the top of the bluff through three tunnels in Mitchell Pass. Views from the summit overlooking the North Platte River Valley are quite impressive.

Scottsbluff is where emigrants felt they left civilization behind and were embarked on harder times ahead. Eroded ruts of wagons are much in evidence. It was through this stretch that cholera seemed most virulent. That dreaded disease killed more people on the trail than any other cause. Accidents took a distant second place. Deaths attributed to Indians, are negligible.

Chip and I rode on to Laramie, WY for the nightly camp.

7-10-90

Located 3 miles south of the town of Laramie, the fort was originally established as a private fur trading fort in 1834. Literally a merry-go-round of trading companies owned it. Built by the Sublette & Campbell Fur Company and called Fort William, it was sold to the Rocky Mountain Fur Company, renamed Fort Lucien, then sold again to Pierre Chouteau who called it Fort John. The "grand old post." saw the sweeping saga of America's westward expansion and Indian resistance to encroachment on their hunting lands. Trappers, traders, missionaries, gold seekers, cowboys and homesteaders left their mark on a place that would become famous in the American West.

The military post of Fort Laramie was founded in 1849 when the army bought old Fort John, and began to build an outpost along the Oregon/California Trail. For many years, the Plains Indians and travelers along the Trail had coexisted peacefully. However, as the number of emigrants increased, tensions between the two cultures developed and to insure the safety of travelers, Congress approved the establishing of forts along the Trail and a special regiment of riflemen to man them. Fort Laramie was the second such fort to be built. It had no walls or structured enclosure, and as an open fort depended on location and troops for security. Needs of emigrant wagon trains were met here. Supplies, repairs, fresh animals, etc., were available at a price.

The Treaty of 1851 between the United States and Plains Indians lasted only 3 years. In 1854, an incident involving a passing wagon train, caused a battle in which several soldiers were killed. This revived the old tensions and major campaigns were mounted against the Plains Tribes. In 1874, the gold rush to the Black Hills of South Dakota violated terms of the Treaty of 1868, inflaming the Sioux who regarded the Black Hills as sacred ground. Under leadership of Crazy Horse and Sitting Bull, they and their allies chose to fight to keep their lands. Fort Laramie was the staging area for troops to engage the Indian Warriors.

Conflict with the Indians had pretty much ended by 1880, and Fort Laramie relaxed into relative Victorian comfort. As with other military installations of the time, officer's quarters were close to lavish with wives being brought from the back east, or acquired locally. Boardwalks were built and trees, flowering shrubs and lawns planted. Ten years later, in 1890, troops marched out of Fort Laramie for the last time. Land and buildings were sold at auction.

The Fort Laramie museum, a National Historic Site operated by the Department of the Interior, is a must see.

Heading west on US-26 on the bank of the North Platte River, the town of Guernsey lies directly on the Trail. In the 1840's this area was known as "the emigrants washtub." Here they washed their clothes, took baths and watered stock. Three miles south of the town of Guernsey are the Guernsey Ruts and Deep Rut Hill. This national monument is the epitome of the trail and its landmarks. The thousands of prairie schooners, carts and wagons drawn by oxen, mules and horses, carved deep into Wyoming sandstone the memory of those pioneers who crossed this country to settle on the West Coast. Wagon masters had been warned that "you will find the road rocky in places and about half way over, there is a sudden turn in the road over rough rocks, which is dangerous to wagons if care is not taken." Where the trail crossed this ridge of soft sandstone, wagons were forced to follow close behind each other. The resulting ruts are worn as deeply as five feet, the most spectacular stretch of ruts of the entire trail.

On the same site is Register Rock. Emigrants inscribed their names on several 'register rocks' along the trail, some to signal to family and friends following, others declaring to all who passed that they had made the trek thus far. Many signatures are quite well preserved. I saw one that read, "The Oregon Wagon Train TEX 1859, SERPA WagonMaster."

At the base of Deep Rut Hill are several graves, most identity unknown, protected by an iron fence. Here too, a well improved gravesite of Lucinda Rawlins. She started her journey from Dayton, Ohio on her way to California and died here in June of 1849. Cause of her death is unknown. Today her grave is marked by an obelisk. The original headstone was vandalized many years ago and presumed to have been thrown into the river. Vandalism is still a problem and the site is not listed on the National Register. By now

Chip and I were tired and stopped to rest and eat under cottonwoods along the North Platte.

After a couple of hours, we took a side trip to Sundance, WY, to renew memories. We enjoyed Sundance very much when we lived here in the sixties. It is a very scenic area, nestled between Devil's Tower and Mount Rushmore in the heart of the Black Hills. This is where Gundi and I adopted our half Arapaho Indian daughter, Karen Elaine. Sundance Kid got his name here and the town really plays it up. Pictures and statues look amazingly like Robert Redford. I visited and had dinner with Bob Uhlrich who worked with me at the Air Force Nuclear Power facility.

7-11-90

Chip and I stayed a second day in Sundance to take in some of the places Gundi and I had seen around here. We rode out to the Vore Buffalo Jump. For over three hundred years, Plains Indians stampeded bison over the rim of a deep sink hole. Without horses, it was the most effective way to procure the animal that was their primary source of food and other materials used in their lifestyle. In 1970, during construction of Interstate 90, excavations unearthed 20 bone layers that extend about 25 feet down. Bones and other artifacts abandoned at the site were buried quickly each year with varves, layers of sediment, that washed into the sinkhole. Materials that would ordinarily erode away are preserved intact, making preservation at this buffalo jump unmatched. This site is now part of the University of Wyoming.

I toured Spearfish, Belle Fourche, Sturgis, and Hulet and visited Devil's Tower. Devil's Tower was a sacred place to several Plains Tribes and is encoded as an important landmark in tribal narratives. Prayer offerings, sweatlodge ceremonies, vision quests and funerals were rituals conducted here. And, of course, the most sacred ritual of all, The Sundance. All but funerals are still performed at this site by Arapaho, Cheyenne, Crow, Kiowa, Shoshone and Lakota. It is their Holy Place.

Cheyenne call it Bear's Lodge. I have read Gunderson's *"Devils Tower – Stories in Stone,"* where he relates that this is where Sweet Medicine died and it is his final resting place. Shaman Sweet Medicine is the great hero of the Cheyenne who brought the Four Sacred Arrows to the tribe. He founded the Cheyenne Warrior Societies, tribal government, special laws and ceremonies. As Sweet Medicine lay dying in a hut by Bear's Lodge, he foretold of the coming of the horse, the disappearance of the old ways and buffalo, to be replaced by "slick animals with split hooves that the people must learn to eat." He told of the coming of white men, called Earth Men who could fly above the earth, take thunder from light, and dig up the earth and drain it until it was dead.

Arapaho, Crow and Lakota Sioux all referred to the Tower as Bear's Tipi, Lair or Lodge. The Kiowa, called it Tree Rock, and origin memories of American Indian people reveal nothing as "bright and remote," as the Kiowa's memories of their days in the Black Hills and at Tree Rock.

I reminded Chip that Prairie falcons nest in the cracks of Devil's Tower. He didn't seem to care. I sure do like this country and its beautiful weather. Not too cold, not too hot. We camped for the night at the Biker's campground in Sturgis. The years we lived in Sundance, I attended all the rallies at Sturgis and rode the area with other bikers on my Harley Sportster. That rally is the largest gathering of Harley Davidson Hogs in the world. I vowed that one day, when I was in the money, I would own a Harley FLT Tour Bike. And one day, I did.

7-12-90

Today, rode down old US-14/16 through Moorcroft, German ranching country, and through Gillette to Spotted Horse. The post office there is closed now, but the restaurant/bar/gas station is still a lively place. The owner is friendly and welcomed Chip at the table with a handful of nuts. He has quite a collection of old saddles and related western gear as well as old cars sitting around in various stages of disrepair.

Buffalo, Wyoming is a pretty historic little town nestled in the foothills of the Big Horn Mountains. The old Occidental Hotel is where Owen Wister's "THE VIRGINIAN, A Horseman of the Plains," got his man. Gary Cooper was the good guy in the 1929 Cecil B. DeMille movie version and James Drury in a later film. A number of pictures based on the novel have been done in Hollywood since 1914. The cover of my book at home features Gary Cooper.

A short drive away is Fetterman's Massacre Site and the infamous "Hole in the Wall" hideout of Butch Cassidy and the Sundance Kid and the rest of the 'wild bunch.' Lots of dude ranches and other outdoor recreation for sportsmen, hunting, fishing, hiking, etc.

From there, through Ten Sleep in the Big Horn Basin. Originally an American Indian rest stop, it was 10 days (ten sleeps) travel from Fort Laramie and the Indian Agency on the Stillwater River in Montana. Numerous archeological sites yield artifacts such as arrow heads, Picto-graphs and Petro-glyphs. Fossil specimen of dinosaurs, plants and sea life are prolific. Big Cedar Fossil Ridge is open to the public for exploration and collection for personal use if you want to build a chair out of dino bones. Ranching is the dominant business, but again, it's a sportsmen's paradise with rock climbing, spelunking, mountain biking and camping. At one time, the Girl Scout National Center West was located at the entrance to Ten Sleep Canyon. It was one of the largest encampments in the world. Something like 15,000 acres. Now part of it is owned by the Nature Conservancy where they have workshops and seminars.

Rode on through Worland and Thermopolis. Hot Springs State Park is at Thermopolis. Lots of hot mineral pools that encourage bathing (for whatever ails you and a fee.) Also a dinosaur center and digs. Wind River Canyon is good trout fishing and other outdoor recreation.

Not far away is small village Shoshoni, named for the Shoshone Indian Tribe that live on the Wind River Reservation. Shoshoni has a continentally arid desert climate and is, in some years, the driest town in the Mountain Time Zone. It is late in the day so Chip and I will camp at Boysen Reservoir for the night. Plan on getting back to the California/Oregon Trail tomorrow.

7-13-90

Cooked bacon, eggs and skillet toast for our breakfast at the campground. Then gassed up in Shoshoni and hit US-20/26 to Casper. This is intermountain high plains country. Bright sunshine, dry short grass and sagebrush, some pronghorn, a few cattle, but the range looks overgrazed. Seems traditional for ranchers to do this. Nice high altitude country that is truly remarkable in its own way.

I picked up the old trail at Fort Casper. Originally founded in 1859 as a trading post and toll bridge for the old Mormon Ferry Crossing of the North Platte River, it was known as the Upper Crossing on the Oregon/California/Mormon Trail. The post was later taken over by the Army under the command of Lt Colonel William Collins, and named the Platte Bridge Station. Following the 1864 Sand Creek Massacre of Cheyenne in Colorado by Col. John M. Chivington, Methodist preacher turned soldier, the military presence was increased to protect emigrants and the telegraph line against raids by Lakota and Cheyenne in the ongoing wars between those tribes and the United States. In 1865, during such a skirmish, Lt. Casper Collins, son Col. Collins, was killed and the post was named Fort Casper. The reconstructed buildings are at the western edge of the present city of Casper. From here follow WY-220 west a few miles along the south side of the North Platte River that brings you to Bessemer Bend on County Road 308. The oldest trail crossing in the Casper area is at this bend. Some emigrants forded the river here to travel on the north side until reaching the Sweetwater Tributary. Others did not cross here, but waited to ford later. The old ford can still be seen a few yards downstream at the modern bridge over the river.

On August 12, 1844, **James Clyman** wrote in his diary, *"Moved up the river 4 miles to a place whare we leave the river and cross over red Bute mountain and encamped a few miles below the Kenyon. The cliffs on this Kenyon are for more than halfway up a fine deep brick red apparently of burned slate and marly dry clay."*

Returning back eastward in 1846, **Clyman** wrote, *"June 23, Early in our saddles and in about 3 hours we met the advance company of oregon Emigration consisting of Eleven wagons nearly opposite the red Butes; when we came in sight of N. Platte we had the Pleasant sight of Beholding the valy to a greate distance dotted with Peopl Horses cattle wagons and Tents their being 30 wagons all Busily engaged in crossing the River which was not found to be fordable and with the poor material they had to make rafts of it took two trips to carry over one wagon with its lading we however ware not long in crossing as we threw our baggage on the returning rafts and swam our animals over and encamped once more in the Buisy hum of our own Language." "June 24 – Down the N Platte and during the day we passed three small companies some for Oregon some for California. It is remarkable how anxious these people are to hear from the*

Pacific country and strange that so many of all kinds and classes of People should sell out comfortable homes in Missouri and Elsewhere pack up and start across such an emmence Barren waste to settle in some new Place of which they have at most so uncertain information, but this is the character of my countrymen."

Still on County road 308, the Trail turns southwest along the east bank of Iron Creek. At the Iron Creek Crossing, this route merges with the trail route from Emigrant Gap. This gap is a shallow pass through a ridge, one of three routes that divided at Fort Casper. This route was especially favored by the Mormon Trains. Emigrant Gap marks the gradual ascent over the Continental Divide at South Pass. Here the BLM interpretive panel reads, *"Ascent gradual. Many singular looking rocks on the south side. Descent rough and crooked. Toward the foot, road very uneven."* **The Latter Day Saints' Emigrants' Guide by William Clayton, St. Louis: 1848** This book has been invaluable to me in tracing landmarks along the Oregon/California Trail. Phyllis found a re-print edited by Stanley Kimball, 1983, in a little St. Louis bookstore that carries used and out of print books.

From this BLM panel, travel west for a mile and a half to the intersection with County Road 12, left to County road 318, and two miles to Poison Springs Clayton's Slough, an area of alkali swamp where, according to **Clayton**, *"The water is nauseous in the extreme. This ought to be avoided as a camping ground – it is a small valley surrounded by very high bluffs. The land exceedingly miry and smells bad."* This was a dry stretch where the emigrants had left the Platte and were headed toward Sweetwater River. Because of the high alkali concentration, though few and far between, springs of water along the trail here are not potable.

The next landmark on this Trail route is the Devil's Backbone. In 1860, **Sir Richard Burton** described it as: *"we descended a steep hill and were shown the Devils'*

Backbone. It is a jagged, broken ridge of huge sandstone boulders tilted up edgewise and running in a line over the crest of a long roll of land, like the vertebrae of some great sea-serpent."

Many emigrant signatures once existed along this stretch of trail but were destroyed, along with several miles of pristine trail ruts, during the construction of an oil pipeline in the 1970's.

For nearly a week, wagon trains traveled through this region of extremely alkaline soil. Animals or people who could not be restrained from drinking from these springs and pools often became ill or died. Approaching Sweetwater River, they reached Saleratus Lake. Saleratus is a naturally occurring sodium bicarbonate substance. The women recognized it as a leavening agent and worked well when added to dough for campfire biscuits and they filled all available containers to carry with them. After the brackish water experience, Willow Springs was a welcome sight. Its sparkling cold water turned this area into a favorite camping site between the North Platte River and Independence Rock. Willow Springs had a small, rough structure that served as relay station for the Pony Express and a post office for emigrants.

Just west of Willow Springs is a low ridge known as Prospect Hill. Climbing this ridge, the wagon trains caught their first sight of the Sweetwater River Valley. From the summit of Prospect Hill, you can clearly see wagon ruts to the north and west, and looking back eastward, the route can be seen back to the North Platte and Casper Mountain. Here was adequate forage and abundant wildlife for fresh meat.

Return to WY-220, (we have been riding pretty much parallel to it all along) to reach Independence Rock, one of the most notable landmarks on the Trail. The name actually comes from a party of fur trappers who camped here on July

4, 1824. This large granite outcropping is 1900 feet long and 700 feet wide and rises 128 feet. From a distance it does indeed look like a huge beached whale. Many travelers carved their names on the great whale. *"engraved on almost every practicable part for the distance of many feet above its base..."* Most are still there. The Jesuit missionary Pierre Jean De Smet called it "The Great Register of the Desert."

Here is the long awaited Sweetwater River that welcomed the wagons to central Wyoming. After the dusty, alkali plains from the Platte, its water was sweet indeed. But what seemed most appealing at first, the gentle, steady, meandering flow, soon turned to frustration. To follow each curve might take a day or more and time was too precious, so they forded the river once, and again... and again... and again...nine times in all. About 5 miles past the first crossing, you arrive at The Devil's Gate. Here the Sweetwater River carved a narrow cleft in the Sweetwater Rocks, about 370 feet deep and 1500 feet long. It is 30 feet wide at the base and 300 feet at the top. Wagons had to travel around the cleft, but frequently emigrants stopped to climb to the top to carve their names and view the surrounding valleys below. They often saw bighorn sheep among the rocks. A marker records, In 1846, Oregon bound emigrant **James Mathers** said, *"this is the most interesting sight we have met on our journey."* Nearly 20 travelers are buried here, though only 1 known grave is marked. Several murders in this region led some to believe this place was truly the devil's gateway to hell.

Shoshone and Arapaho Tribes attribute Devil's Gate to an evil beast with enormous tusks (possibly mammoths) that once roamed the land, prevented the Indians from hunting and camping here. Eventually, the Indians decided to kill the beast and warriors shot it with many arrows. Enraged the great beast tore a hole in the mountains and escaped.

This area is best seen from the BLM Interpretive Center at a turn off on WY-220. Trail ruts are visible here, as well as Martin's Cove at the entrance to the Mormon Handcart Visitor's Center, described in detail there. I quote randomly, 'In early 1856, Mormon converts began the long trek from England to Zion. They traveled by ship, train, wagon and finally handcart west across the plains. The Martin Company left Iowa City late in the season, and unable to afford the toll at Renshaw's Bridge, forded the North Platte in bitterly cold weather. The next day, October 19th, a blizzard dropped temperatures to well below zero. Within 8 miles beyond the Platte, 56 members froze to death. When Brigham Young learned the party was still on the trail, he sent rescue parties from Salt Lake City to assist. By the time the rescuers reached the Martin Party, they were spread out over 60 miles of trail, from Red Buttes to Martin's Cove.' **Daniel Jones** wrote; *"There were old men tugging their carts, sometimes loaded with sick women and children, women pulling along sick husbands, little children six to eight years old struggling through mud and snow…the provisions we had amounted to almost nothing among so many people. The men seemed to be dying faster than the women and children."*

With the help of rescuers, The Martin Company took refuge in a sheltered pocket on the south side of the Sweetwater Mountains, now known as Martin's Cove. Nearly a fourth of the 576 members of the Martin Company died before arriving in Salt Lake City on November 30, 1856. The actual site of Martin's Cove is still owned by the BLM, but surrounding land is now owned by the Church of Jesus Christ of the Latter Day Saints.

Chip and I returned to Independence Rock, BLM public land, and set up camp for the night at the edge of the Rock. A can of pork and beans with wieners and a bag of potato chips tasted pretty good. Even instant Taster's Choice Coffee was not bad.

7-14-90

Following US-285, the Oregon/California/Mormon Trail is to the north of the highway at Split Rock and south of the Sweetwater River. The Sweetwater Valley has three distinctive granite landmarks; Independence Rock, The Devil's Gate and Split Rock. Decades before wagon trains went this way, Split Rock had guided travelers. Split Rock is the "gun sight notch" in the Rattlesnake Mountain Range. Rising some 1000 feet above the prairie, it aimed emigrants directly at South Pass, still more than 75 miles away. This region offered them a short respite on their long journey. Split Rock Station is located a short distance west between Cranner Rock and the south bank of the Sweetwater River in what is now a hay field. It was a Pony Express, stagecoach and telegraph station in the early 1860's. The crude log building and pole corral are now part of a private ranch. In 1862, 50 soldiers from the 6th Ohio Regiment were encamped here to protect wagon trains from the Indians. Legend says soldiers built a tunnel between the post and the river so they could get water without being seen.

Three Crossings Canyon in the Rattlesnake Hills near this post, confronted the emigrants with three difficult river crossings within two miles of each other. If they chose not to make the crossings, they could follow the 'deep sand' alternate south of the Sweetwater. Buried in the Three Crossings area is Private Tribbett, a 19 year old soldier of the Ohio 6th. He died of appendicitis on December 14, 1862. This is memorable because of a grave marker photo taken in 1870. **Private A. Barleon** wrote to Tribbett's sister, *"We made a coffin of such lumber as we had, and dressed him in his best clothes, laid a blanket around him and tucked a blanket around the coffin to make it look a little better. The escort fired three rounds over his grave."* Reproductions of photographs of the grave taken by William Henry Jackson in the summer of 1870 show a wooden board that indicates Tribbett was **"Killed by Indians."** It is believed these photos were altered to sensationalize the death. The original marker, 1862, is part of the Fort Casper Museum and makes no mention of Indians.

Three Crossings Canyon is now owned by Western Nuclear Corporation and not accessible to the public.

Okay. We talked about 'deep sand' as an alternate route for wagon trains. So, having taken this route, those travelers now found a grassy swamp awaiting. Just below it, by digging down sometimes just a few inches, they found a bed of solid, clear ice. This is known as Ice Slough, and according to **Gregory Franzwa**, (Francois) *"was one of those absolutely delightful interludes that somehow seemed to crop up just as the incessant slogging west was putting us in the lowest of spirits."* Actually, the Ice Slough is a small tributary that drains into the Sweetwater. Various marsh grasses and tufted sedge plants form a patchwork of surface plant life. Water flowing underneath this insulating peat-like vegetation, freezes solid in winter and remains frozen into early summer. In the middle of a hot, dusty trek, travelers found ice a real treat and it became a favorite camping site. They dug up blocks of ice and stored them in their water barrels to provide cold water for the long stretch ahead. Chip and I decided it was the place for lunch, though today's irrigation diversions have left the slough almost dry and for sure no ice.

The emigrants crossing the main route crossed the Sweetwater for the 5th time about eight miles west of Three Crossings Canyon. Those who chose the Deep Sand Route avoided Three Crossings as well as 5th Crossing. After 5th Crossing, the trail leaves the river for about 16 miles until it reaches 6th Crossing, where all routes crossed. The 7th and 8th Crossings of the Sweetwater are about seven miles east of Rocky Ridge. These two crossings, about a half mile apart, served trains that chose the river in order to avoid the climb over a steep, sandy hill. Ruts over the Sand Route hill are deep and well preserved. The 5th and 6th Crossings are on private land. The 7th and 8th are on BLM lands.

Rocky Ridge is a stretch of trail that caused Wagon Trains no end of grief. They ascended this barren ridge after leaving the Sweetwater Valley en route to South Pass. The trail ascends about 700 feet in two miles through a rugged boulder strewn path. A monument to another Mormon Handcart Company sits on Rocky Ridge. In this company, 21 people froze to death here. The full stretch of trail runs about twelve miles, across two high ridge shelves, crosses Strawberry Creek and passes the old ghost town of Lewiston. The rock cuts left by wagon wheels are among the most dramatic trail remnants left on the westward trails. Signs on US-287 warn extreme caution is necessary to reach the ridge itself and should be taken by only 4WD vehicles and NOT tourists traveling alone, so I chose not to put myself, Chip, or the Harley through this. Instead we went to the Sweetwater Station Rest Area on the BLM turnoff of US-287 that offers a good overlook.

The almost imperceptible crest in the Rocky Mountain Range is the most significant site on the westward emigrant trails. Here at South Pass, they crossed the Continental Divide, going from the drainage basin if the Atlantic Ocean to that of the Pacific Ocean. Now they could legitimately say they had entered Oregon Territory.

Of course South Pass was known to the native inhabitants of this area for centuries. Nonetheless, its "discovery" is almost always attributed to the Astorians of 1812 who, under the leadership of Robert Stuart crossed here heading east with dispatches for John Jacob Astor. Twelve years later it was 'rediscovered' by fur trappers, including Jedediah Smith and Thomas Fitzpatrick. Captain Benjamin Bonneville took the first wagons west over the summit in 1832 and ten years later, Lt. John Charles Fremont set the stage for the great migration beginning in 1842 by announcing it could be crossed without any "toilsome ascents." Two markers are on the summit. One marks it as "The Old Oregon Trail," the other dedicated to the first two women who crossed on July 4, 1836. From Junction US-285 and WY-28, follow 28 that approaches the trail at the Pass, but crosses a few miles to the southwest. The trail crossing can be seen from the highway. Probably the worst part of the emigrants' journey still lay ahead.

I did not ride the Seminoe Cutoff between Rocky Ridge and South Pass, but it has an interesting history. It remained south of the Sweetwater River, avoiding four of the crossings and the infamous Rocky Ridge. Basil LaJeunesse, a trapper called Seminoe, gave the cutoff its name. He married a Shoshone Indian woman and lived with her band. The cutoff leaves the main Oregon/California Trail at Warm Springs a few miles from the 6th Crossing of the Sweetwater. The main disadvantage was lack of water, but a few springs along the way was enough for small trains and it was the preferred route of the Mormon Companies. It rejoins the main trail a few miles east of South Pass.

What may be one of the most dramatic sites remaining on the trails is in the middle of an open sagebrush plain where the trails diverge. Emigrants had to decide whether to stay on the main route and head toward Fort Bridger, or veer right and cross the Little Colorado Desert on the Greenwood Sublette Cutoff. This saved about 46 miles, all waterless. On WY 28, a few miles from the BLM Interpretive overlook at South Pass, a 1956 marker proclaims this divergent site as "The Parting of the Ways. This marks a fork in the trail, right to Oregon, left to Utah and California." In 1988, the Oregon-California Trails Association erected another marker next to the first which correctly states that the true parting of the ways lies another nine and a half miles to the west. This site is referred to as the "False Parting," and the real site is the "True Parting." At True Parting, the eye can follow the divergent trails for miles. But wait a minute. This is not entirely accurate either. Either branch would lead to wherever you are going. Remember Yogi Berra said, "When you come to a Y in the road, take it.' Same here. Those who needed supplies took the left fork to Fort Bridger. Since this was also the route to Utah, Mormons took the road left, as did many California trains that traveled with their new Oregon-bound friends as far as the middle of Idaho. But the Parting of the Ways marks a spot where many bid farewell to friends they would never see again.

Some of the California trains went south from here by the Hastings Cutoff, an alternate route as proposed by Lansford Hastings. In 1845, he published a guide describing the trail in this way: "The most direct route for the California emigrants, would be to leave the Oregon route, about two hundred miles east of Fort Hall; thence bearing West-Southwest, to Salt Lake City; and thence continuing down to the bay of San Francisco, by the route just described."

In 1846, between 60 and 75 wagons traveled with Hastings on his Cutoff. They endured a difficult descent down Weber Canyon, a waterless route of 80 miles over the Great Salt Lake Desert, and a long detour around the Ruby Mountains. Nonetheless, they arrived in California without loss of life or livestock. The Donner Party that followed close behind did not fare so well, reaching the Cutoff a few days too late to join the initial train. Pioneering an alternate route to avoid Weber Canyon, they were delayed farther by road building through the Wasatch Mountains, and arrived at the pass just as an early winter storm closed in. Snowbound in the Sierra Nevada, many died and some resorted to cannibalism to survive. The following year, Brigham Young led his Mormon emigrants along the Hastings Cutoff, making improvements to the trail as they went, so subsequent Mormon travelers could make the journey safely.

Chip and I chose not to venture along this route and camped the night on the river bank among the willows of the Green River, very near where John Wesley Powell embarked on his famous exploration of the Colorado River in 1869. Ham's Fork of the Green River, near present day Granger, is the site of the fur trade rendezvous in 1834. Between 1825 and 1840, sixteen fur trade rendezvous were held in the Green River Valley. A favorite site for trading companies and trappers to meet, these camps spread over many miles. Most mountain men brought their Indian women along. Girls and women were bargained for as easily as rich beaver furs, in exchange for beads and guns. Besides, these mates were much easier to get along with and considerably more subservient than white women in such a nomadic lifestyle.

7-15-90

The trail can be crossed again about the junction of WY-28 and 372. I picked up the trail at Fort Bridger. Jim Bridger, along with his partner Louis Vasquez, established their first trading post at the Black Fork of the Green River. Fur trade had pretty much died out by 1843, and Bridger predicted that the location "promises fairly" for major development of the West to pass its doors. Efforts were directed toward inducing customers to stop for supplies and repairs. It welcomed mountain men, Indians, westward emigrants and Mormon pioneers, the Pony Express, the Overland Stage, the Union Pacific Railroad and the U.S. Army. Abandoned in 1890, the buildings were sold at auction and moved to become private homes, barns and bunk houses for local ranches. What remained at the original site fell into disrepair until the 1930's, when restoration began. It is a Wyoming Historical Landmark and Museum. There is an admission fee, worth the purchase.

Another destination on the Sublette Greenwood Cutoff was Fort Hall in Idaho, but most chose to take the longer trail to Fort Hall and avoid those Cutoff miles with no water. Following the Bear River in Idaho, the Oregon Trail crossed the Thomas Fork tributary. This was a hard ford until two entrepreneurs built bridges which helped those who had the dollar per wagon toll to cross. Here too, travelers encountered Big Hill, a rough ascent and very steep descent. Journals from emigrants can be read at the Montpelier Interpretive Center.

Theodore Talbot, September 7, 1843. *"We went a few miles farther when we had to cross a very high hill, which is said to be the greatest impediment on the whole route from the United States to Fort Hall. The ascent is very long and tedious, but the descent is still more abrupt and difficult."*

Margaret A. Frink, July 6, 1850, *"We started at six o'clock, forded Thomas Fork, and turning to the west, came to a high spur we were compelled to climb. The distance is seven miles, and we were five hours in crossing. Part of the way I rode on horseback, the rest I walked. The descent was very long and steep. All the wheels of the wagon were tied fast, and slid along the ground. At one place the men held it back with ropes and let it down slowly."*

Fort Hall was built by Nathaniel Wyeth in 1834 as a supply center for fur traders and Indians. In 1838, he sold the post to Hudson's Bay Company and it began operating as a fort, though it continued to serve as a supply stop until 1856. The original site is on Fort Hall Indian Reservation and permission is required to visit it. Not only is it hard to find, but nothing remains but a chunk of wall inside a fenced enclosure. The roads are washboard and hard on the Harley, and I did not try. At Pocatello is an excellent replica and museum well worth seeing.

The City of Pocatello is named for Chief Pocatello of the Shoshoni Tribe, located along the Portneuf River where it emerges from the mountains onto the Snake River Plain. The city has a number of camping parks and I am pretty tired. Chip and I will take a break to shower, do some laundry, and wash the motorcycle. I will not follow the Oregon Trail farther.

Chapter 11

This is My Country, Land that I Love

7-16-90

I took I-15 from Pocatello to Salt Lake City. I have some concern about Chip in big cities. Small towns are no problem, but traffic noise and general commotion can be a major factor. Usually I leave him in a saddle bag, but this doesn't make him happy. So I stopped at a small pet store on the outskirts of Salt Lake City and bought a soft-sided hamster cage to fasten on the buddy seat. It has mesh screens so he can see out, but zips up to keep him inside. Also a built-in water dish and food tray. Why didn't I think of it sooner?

Having followed much of the Mormon Trail across the country, I felt inclined to circle Temple Square and see the ultimate destination. Unless you are a member of the Church of Jesus Christ of the Latter Day Saints, you are not allowed inside the temple, and with the distinction of being a spurned outsider, I was not tempted to go in anyway.

The temple edifice itself is quite magnificent in the neo-gothic style of many cathedrals world wide. It took the faithful 40 years to construct; 1853-1893. The Tabernacle does allow visitors on guided tours. It is the home of the famous Tabernacle Choir and known for its acoustic qualities. I have some records of the Choir that are really great listening and I enjoy them very much. In the same complex is the Museum of Church History with exhibits of covered wagons, log cabins and other memorabilia from the Trail and a copy of the Book of Mormon. Parking is at a premium price and hard to come by, so I chose just to ride the Harley around the square.

Following US-40 east out of Salt Lake City, we camped in a small roadside campground at the foot of Mt. Olympus in the Wasatch Mountains. This is the highest peak near Salt Lake City. I found it somewhat amusing that a mountain with such a pagan name rose over the Mormon Temple.

7-17-90

Early the next morning, I fixed breakfast, packed up the tent and folded Chip's new hamster carrier into a saddlebag. No need for it through the country we are traveling now, since we are on our way across the Wasatch Mountain Range and into the Uintas. These are really good mountains. They are usually considered to be the western edge of the Rocky Mountains, but are not especially high compared to the Colorado Rockies. Mount Nebo, at the southern end of the Wasatch Range, is 11,928 feet. But being constructed by glacial action, the Wasatch display very rugged scenery that compares well with higher ranges. It is from the high quality granite in these mountains, that the Mormon Temple is built.

As soon as we got east of the Uintas, we were in rim rock country of the Colorado Plateau, with juniper, sagebrush and the like. It is hot and dry. I stopped at the Hilltop Café, way out in the boonies, for a super sized glass of iced tea, and made a note in my journal to write a few pages about the Colorado Plateau this evening when we camp.

Around Vernal, Utah, the valleys are watered by irrigation from creeks and rivers that run through. Here US-40 is wide, beautifully curved and easy to ride. Vernal has a good museum featuring primarily dinosaur fossils found in such abundance in this area.

Craig, CO is at the junction of US-40 and CO-13, the midpoint between Salt Lake City and Denver. The Yampa River offers sports fishing, I am assuming various species of trout, and the surrounding area has a lot of wildlife. We saw elk, deer, wild horses, sandhill cranes and eagles. I understand there are interesting petro-glyphs in the hills. We decided to camp the night on the Yampa and hope cougars kept their distance.

★★★★

Colorado Plateau

The Utah rim rock country marks the northwestern edge of the Colorado Plateau, a major geological shaper of the Western United States. If I followed this rim far enough, I would edge the Rio Grande Rift, walk along the North Rim of the Grand Canyon and stand on the Mogollon Rim in Arizona. A remarkable feature of the Colorado Plateau is its stability. Little faulting or folding has affected this thick tectonic crustal block in the last 600 million years or so, although it has lifted and dropped a number of times, creating and draining inland seas. Tectonic blocks surrounding this Plateau have separated and collided to thrust up High Rockies, such as the Sangre de Christos, all around it. Scattered throughout the Plateau, lower sub-ranges of the Southern Rockies formed when this block dropped and other rifting blocks folded over the top.

Precambrian history of the Colorado Plateau is best seen in the Grand Canyon where exposed strata span nearly 2 billion years. The oldest rock at the Colorado River level, is igneous and metamorphic. This strata, known as the Vishnu Basement, formed some 1950 to 1680 million years ago.

Erosion surface on this basement is sedimentary and basalt flow, about 1250 to 750 millions years ago, and in turn these flows were uplifted and split.

Throughout the Paleozoic Era, tropical seas periodically inundated the Colorado Plateau region. Layers of limestone, sandstone and shale were deposited and accumulated, so when the sea retreated as the Plateau uplifted, stream deposits and sand dunes were laid down and older layers removed by erosion. Most of the Plateau landscape is related in appearance and history. Sometimes referred to as "Red Rock Country," this has lead to the greatest concentration of National Parks in the United States. Among them, Grand Canyon, Zion, Brice, Capitol Reef, Canyonlands, Arches, and the Petrified Forest. National Monuments of the Plateau are, Dinosaur, Hovensweep, Waptki, Grand Staircase-Escalante, and Colorado National Monument. One should never dismiss the wonderful Monument Valley formations, mostly in the Navajo Nation of the Four Corners: Arizona, Colorado, Utah and New Mexico.

★★★★

There is so much more to the continuing saga of the Colorado Plateau Region. A fascinating story I would love to tell, but I am tired and Chip wants dinner.

7-18-90

Today we rode US-40 to Walden. With a population of around 300, it is the county seat of Jackson County. The welcome sign approaching town says it is "The Moose Viewing Capital of Colorado." Okay. I think a few such animals were brought here from Canada some years ago to adapt and reproduce for big game hunting and relieve the overpopulation in whatever Province they came from. They must still be protected (slow reproducers maybe) so can be photographed but not killed.

Walden is in the majestic mountains of North Park. It is unincorporated and once called Sagebrush, but renamed in honor of a local postmaster, Marcus Aurelius Walden. I picked that up from a brochure in Craig. His parents must have been readers of Roman History or Philosophy. On through Walden to Granby.

Granby, Colorado is in a beautiful, wide valley of Rocky Mountain National Park between Grand Lake and Winter Park. The Continental Divide borders the valley on the east and here on the Western Slope, the headwaters of the Colorado River begin. A dam at Granby Reservoir holds the river back, and pumps lift water into Shadow Mountain Lake. From there it flows into Grand Lake, where the Alva B. Adams Tunnel carries it through the Divide to the Eastern Slope. There it empties into the South Platte River. So the Colorado River feeds water, not only to Nevada, Arizona and California, but as far east as Nebraska. Pretty powerful river, ain't it?

On to Kremmling which lies at the confluence of Muddy Creek, Blue River and the Colorado River in Grand County. Some spectacular mesa rock formations here, apparently glacial remains. It is located at the junction of US-40 and CO-9. We stopped at the general store, the first building in Kremmling (1884), to pick up some lunch and ate beside the crystal clear water of Muddy Creek. I gassed up the Harley and we took CO-9 south along the Blue River and rode through Breckenridge, Fairplay, and Hartsel to US-50 at Cañon City. I headed back to CO-67 to ride north into Phantom Canyon, a haunt of my youth. This gravel road follows the route of the Florence and Cripple Creek Railroad built in 1894 by Spencer Penrose, owner of the Cash on Delivery Gold Mine in Cripple Creek, to carry ore to smelters in Florence. Penrose is also the millionaire that 'e Broadmoor Hotel in Colorado Springs, and the ,wn of Penrose where I graduated from high school, is named for him. Phantom Canyon's bridges and tunnels are a visual link to the past glory of the goldfields in the Cripple Creek and Victor area. The road conditions keep the Harley at a slow crawl, but no matter. I love this place where I spent so many days prospecting for gold when our family lived at Brush Hollow Ranch near the town of Penrose. I even staked a claim a few hundred yards off the road along a dry creek bed. I had found a beryl crystal buried there, a sure sign of gold ore. Because I never worked it, my claim ran out 25 years later. Oh, well. Chip was indifferent when I told him about it. We camped for the night at a campground at the lower end of the canyon.

7-19-90 to 7-21-90

Badly in need of a few days rest, I rode east along interstate highways to Springfield, MO, to Pittsburg and Florence's farm.

7-23-90 to 7-31.90

Rejuvenated and with the Harley spruced up and in top condition again, Chip and I took off for Torrance, California to visit with Vivian. Chip seemed glad to be on the road again and we had an interesting ride with few stops, but much enjoyment from the mixed prairie/woods of central Missouri, the Flint Hills of Kansas, classic cattle country of Western Kansas/Eastern Colorado, irrigated river valleys, semi-arid uplands, alfalfa fields, melons, onions, Colorado mountains, Utah, colossal canyons, dry lake beds, hot south wind, dust from the lake beds, Nevada, cool mornings, scenic high desert, cedar, juniper, sagebrush, and wild horses. I made one stop in Nevada, just to see what I could see. I had a dream once a few years back, that I was in Tonopah, Nevada. It was a wild west town of cowboys, Indians and fancy ladies. What was it like, really? I detoured off US-50A at Ely and took US-6 to Tonopah. Indians and fancy ladies, perhaps, but no cowboys. "Queen of the Silver Camps" is its tag line. For centuries, Indian tribes camped at Tonopah Springs. So there's the Indian part. In May of 1900, rancher Jim Butler spent a night here at the spring, and in the morning, found his mule gone wandering. Eventually he caught the beast near an outcrop of rock that seemed laden with silver. He took samples to an assayer, who said they were worthless, mostly iron, and threw them in the back of his own tent. But suspicious Butler demanded their return and later at his ranch in Monitor Valley, set them in the window sill. Tasker Oddie, (later Governor of Nevada,) came visiting and offered to pay for another assay. Butler gave him a quarter interest of the assay. Oddie took a sample to assayer Gayhart and offered him a quarter of his quarter to run the assay. Turned out it ran about $600 a ton. So that was the end of the Indians and the beginning of a mining boom and fancy ladies in Tonopah. Hm-mm-m. Anyway, Chip, now it is pretty much a ghost town with tourist businesses, gambling halls and …fancy ladies?

Continued on US-6 out of Tonopah and through the California Mojave Desert past Death Valley to Bishop, CA. From there, US-395 to CA-14, to I-5. Hot and dry, though much of the comfort level has to do with time of day. I-5 in metro LA to Freeways-405 and 110 to Sepulveda Blvd. in Torrance and the Pine Tree Apartments with Chip securely zipped in his hamster cage. Vivian loves Los Angeles. I don't ask why.

8-1-90

Today is my 60th birthday. I left Chip secure in his cage in her apartment and locked the Harley Davidson FLT on the patio.

vian took me to the harbor area of San Pedro for the day. We had lunch at a little sidewalk café overlooking the Pacific and the cliff where streets and houses fell off during the 1931 Long Beach earthquake. Broken streets and remnants of foundations, brick walls and gardens still rest at the bottom of the cliff. It is known locally as The Sunken City. It is quite possible do go down there and explore, but we didn't. Instead we went tide-pooling below Point Fermin Lighthouse. Sea anemones, sea cucumbers and viciously spiny urchins abound there. Saw a few small barracuda sharks. I don't get my feet wet in the Pacific that often and it was fun. We dried off on the sand at Cabrillo Beach and watched the pelicans. Sis sure loves pelicans. We saw a couple of ARCO tankers from Prudhoe Bay come into the harbor. Lots of small sail boats and fishing boats coming and going. We dragged unimportant things out of our past to talk about. Finally, Vivian said, "Okay, Warren, what is really on your mind?"

"Sis, for 20 years I have begged you to come to Alaska to see me. I wanted so much to show you my beautiful state. But you never came. I think I can show it to you through my eyes, if you'll do me a favor. I'm keeping a journal about my travels around North America. I'm not finished yet, but when I am, would you take it and do something with it? I'd even like it to get published someday. I think that's possible. But I need you to make it more interesting than just the log I'm writing. What do you think? Will you?"

She thought a while. "What are you going to add?"

"Well, if I can keep this cancer in remission, I want to ride again next summer. I still have to tour the southern tier of states. I want to see the Southeast and Deep South. I want to scope out Lake Charles and Lake Arthur in Louisiana where Mom was born and spent her childhood. I'd like to cross into the East Texas Piney Woods, go up through southern Arkansas, cross Oklahoma to see the outcome of the Indian Nation. See if Darlington is still there and what might be left from your birthplace. I want to look into the border history in southern New Mexico and Arizona, and then I really do want to ride around in the Yuma area. That's where you come in, Sis. Could you drive down to Yuma and meet me to ride those byways? The formations are so surreal. Dome Rock Road and Mohawk Valley, Yuma Territorial Prison and River Crossing, Old Fort Yuma are all a must see. Then we'd ride north along the Colorado River from Yuma and see the old ruins and other history all the way to the Grand Canyon. What do you think, Sis? Could you take some vacation time and put that in your plan?"

"I think that's a splendid idea, Buddy Boy." She reached out and squeezed my hand. "I think we ought to do exactly that."

"And what about the journal?"

"Okay. I promise. Just for you, Warren."

8-2-90 to 8-5-90

Took I-15 as far as Fallon, NV then US-50 to Delta, UT. US-6 is usually more scenic, I think, but going through the Virgin River Gorge where the 15 cuts through Arizona, was almost as much a spiritual experience as the Grand Canyon. Old gods live in places like this. And from Fallon to Delta was an interesting segment. Cooler now than when I was going west last week. The terrain between Salina and Green River, UT is quite beautiful, with stunning castellated rock formations. CO-13 from Rifle, CO through Meeker.

There is a lot of Colorado history here. This was Ute Indian country. They called themselves "The Blue Sky People" and claimed the Rocky Mountains as their homeland. Plains tribes pretty much left them alone. They seemed not particularly neighborly. Chief Ouray tried his best to keep the peace with the United States Government, but the natives were restless. Some had been herded onto the White

River Reservation on the Western Slope, where Nathanial Meeker had been appointed Agent. His idea was to convert the nomadic 'savages' to God fearing farmers. Not much luck with such unpopular ideas. He was warned that the Utes were furious with his reforms. Those horse loving Indians whose favorite pastime was racing their ponies, built a race track for just that purpose. Meeker ordered the track plowed under, turned into farmland and told the Utes they had too many horses, to kill some.

Well, that did it. Meeker got in a fist fight with the Ute that owned the race track and wired for military assistance. After all, he had been assaulted by an Indian, driven from his home, and severely injured. So here came the troops again, to correct the natives. 200 soldiers led by Major Thornburgh were met by a group of Utes about 50 miles from the Agency, who said they wanted a peace conference with Meeker, and Thornburgh and 5 soldiers were invited to attend. The rest were to stay away on a hill assigned by the Utes, because they did not want a repeat of the Sand Creek Massacre where Colonel John Chivington killed a whole Cheyenne camp. Thornburgh didn't listen and just kept advancing. Not a good idea. These were Utes, not Cheyenne. At Mill Creek the angry warriors ambushed the troops and killed all the officers including Thornburgh, turned on the Agency, killed Meeker along with 8 men, and took women captives to secure their safety as they fled. So that is known in Colorado History books as "The Meeker Massacre." Shoe on the other foot, so to speak.

Now, no Indians, just a lot of coal mining that seems to have revived the community since I passed through here in 1969. I rode on through Craig and Walden and to Laramie and Lusk WY. Beautiful country. Finally to McCook, NE where I am catching up on my journal. I will head back to Alaska from here. I want to leave the Harley Davidson FLT at home and drive my Ford Granada down and leave it at Florence's place for the winter. Something tells me I may need it for next summer. A gut feeling I will not ignore. I will fly back to Anchorage from KC. Then to Hawaii for a couple of months with Gundi and my granddaughter, Meghan. That is the plan for now. I am very tired.

Chapter 12

The Last Ride

Vivian Zanini

This is the end of Warren's journal. In September, 1990, he drove his 1977 Ford Granada to the lower 48, stopped in Wichita to see Ralph and then on to Pittsburg, MO to Florence's farm where he took the battery out of his car, jacked it onto blocks and covered it with a tarp, leaving it behind Mom's and Dad's old house there. Dale took him to the airport in Kansas City and he flew home to Anchorage. I don't think he and Connie went to Hawaii that year, because he wrote me often and phoned the first Sunday of every month.

In a Birthday card:

"October, 1, 1990.

Dear Sis,

The 4th is your birthday and I wish you a happy one. A tidbit of information. I know you have always said Mom told you the mid-wife who attended your birth in Darlington, OK was a Choctaw Indian called Big Belly Woman, and that she took your navel and buried it on Indian land. That is altogether possible, because, as you know, it was Andrew Jackson's plan that all of Oklahoma was supposed to be one big Indian Nation, a reservation for all tribes of the United States. It was the end of a trail of tears, not just for the Cherokee, but all other tribes as well. At any rate, I wrote the El Reno, Oklahoma Chamber of Commerce and got quite a bit of historical literature. Darlington was the tribal Agency headquarters for the Cheyenne/Arapaho, established in 1870 by Indian Agent Brinton Darlington, a Quaker appointed by President Grant. It was a stop on the old Chisholm Trail, also site of the Arapaho School. The post office was built in 1873. The Cheyenne School was opened in 1871. The Mennonites had a mission there, too. I doubt this is where Dad taught. More likely it would have been a small school for the white agency kids. But by the time you were born in 1931, Indians of all tribes were pretty much integrated throughout the state, so Big Belly Woman could have been Choctaw. But the agency at Darlington is still Cheyenne/Arapaho. The State Game Farm is there now, and Redlands Community College (an Indian College as the name implies) where the old Cheyenne School dormitory was. At El Reno, in 1901, Kiowa and Comanche lands were distributed by lottery during the Oklahoma Land Rush. So much for the "Indian Nation." But good old redneck Andy Jackson, 'the only good Injun is a dead Injun', and the US Gub'met didn't have the gumption to withhold mineral rights, so the Indians held the oil rights, took the royalties, and got rich in spite of the Feds. The Cherokee made out like bandits, richer than even in Georgia, but without the black slaves they kept back east. The Choctaw aren't exactly poverty stricken either. Maybe it is the "Indian Nation" after all. So that's what I learned about Darlington.

Have a Happy Birthday, sis.

Love, Warren."

In a phone call late October, Warren told me the asbestos tumors in his plural cavity had begun a rapid increase in growth. His months of remission seemed to be at an end. Traditional radiation or chemotherapy were pointless, and his only recourse to pain remedy was having the fluid that accumulated below his lungs, drained out, as had been done before his trial with Chelation Therapy. He said the procedure was more painful than the fluid itself, but he knew it was the only way to function semi-normally in any way. He did not think he would be able to ride across the southern tier of states the next summer after all.

He had received some literature from Louisiana and he would write me about Calcasieu Parish when he got to feeling a little better. He assured me Chip was fine. Getting a little bit long in the tooth and would be hibernating soon. Gundi was well, and said hello.

November, 17, 1990.

"Dear Vivian,

We are having a period of intense Northern Lights right now. Wish you could see them. Remember that winter we could see them as far south as Elbert? After Dad told us what they were, you and I would bundle up in Grandma Garrison's handmade comforters and sit on the front porch and watch them with such wonder. That was nothing to what we see here in Alaska. I am enclosing a postcard of how spectacular they are.

As far as Louisiana is concerned, Lake Charles Historical Society sent some documentation that includes very little of the period at the turn of the century when Mom was born in nearby Lake Arthur. I did see that it is the area where the Acadians settled, and several streets and places such as parks are called "Evangeline." As a matter of fact, Lake Charles is the western point of 22 parishes that make up present day Acadiana. Wish I could scope that out more, since I have seen the Canadian side of the story. Presently Lake Charles is given over to the oil industry.

Lake Arthur is all about the "Lakers" sports teams, an. the Holiness Campmeeting grounds are still alive and v. after 113 years. I think that is probably where Mom's brothers Oran and Mahlon found salvation. And if I recall, they finally got Mom and Uncle Orville saved as well. Lake Arthur hasn't been in Calcasieu Parish since 1910.

Center, Texas is still central to the East Texas Piney Woods, now the Sabine National Forest. Clear cutting is evident along the railroad beds, but still looks beautiful from brochure photos. Victoria, Texas, is way south, not far from Houston. I think I might as well leave the family ancestry stories to Cousin Margaret Roark, who seems to have taken up that cause.

Love, Warren

From this point, further correspondence between us did not concern his travels, but were more philosophical in nature as he began preparing himself for his transition out of this Earth life. In the summer of 1991, Warren and Chip rode his Harley Davidson to St. Louis to see Phyllis, to Pittsburg, MO to see Florence and to Wichita to see Ralph. Leaving Wichita, he realized he was very ill and rode back to Pittsburg. There he stored his Harley under a tarp in Florence's garage and turned Chip loose in the woods. He and Dale got his Ford Granada ready to go and Florence agreed to drive him to California to see me. They traveled on I-40, and approaching Albuquerque, NM, Warren was in such pain they detoured to a hospital there for him to get the fluid sucked out of his plural cavity. Florence told me later she was so grateful the hospital posted blue signs along the Interstate directing them to it. She said she wore dark glasses because she was crying all the way across the country. She drove until they reached I-15 in California, then Warren took over and drove on to my place in Torrance. He found a storage unit for his Ford, and left me the keys. They stayed with me one day. I took both of them to LAX, Warren to fly home to Anchorage and Florence to fly to Kansas City where Dale picked her up to drive home to Pittsburg.

In the spring of 1992, Ralph flew to Anchorage and arranged to buy the Ford, flew down to Los Angeles and picked up the car to drive to Wichita. He said if I wanted to see Warren alive, I'd better get to Anchorage really soon. Warren had not told any of us how close to the end he was. He did not want us to come see him the way he looked. How he looked was of no concern to me. I called Florence and Phyllis, and Phil said she did not want to go to Anchorage. She preferred to yield to Warren's wishes. Florence met me in Seattle in mid June, and we flew to Anchorage to bid farewell to our big brother and wish him well on his journey out of this phase of his life. He kept his sense of humor to the end. Florence asked him, "Did anyone ever tell you, you look like Sean Connery?" He laughed. "No, they tell me Sean Connery looks like me."

That last visit was when he told me of the ladder and made his final request that I write his journal story.

Florence returned to Los Angeles with me for a few days. The second day with me, a minor earthquake shook L.A. She decided to go home.

Warren passed away on July 1, Florence's and Phyllis's birthday. A few weeks later, Warren's friend John drove his SUV from Anchorage to Pittsburg to pick up the Harley Davidson. When he and Dale took the tarp off, they found a little bit of dried up gray stripped fur and bone lying on the buddy seat. Dale buried Chip at the foot of a black walnut tree in the back yard.

Afterword

Footprints

> "We will grieve not, rather find
> Strength in what is left behind."
>
> William Wordsworth, "Ode on Intimations of Immortality"

I will include only two short passages from the time Warren and I were corresponding regularly in 1990. My Christmas letter to family and friend in early December, 1990, was a fictional style story titled *"Musing With a Pelican at Point Vicente."* I based it on an old one-legged pelican I talked to near the lighthouse at Point Vicente on the Pacific coast on the Palos Verde Peninsula above San Pedro.

I said, *"Our treasures are the successes and failures that enhance our growth. We guard them as our most precious possessions, because they are what make us what we are. We set a Griffin at the door to keep them safe. We can't let trash be thrown in."* The pelican heard the door slam shut on her private treasures. She came to stand next to him at the rail. For a long time, she looked out over the vastness of the ocean. Then she said very softly, *"My brother Warren came to see me this summer. For his Birthday."*

"You love him very much, don't you?"

"I adore him." She retreated into her own treasure house. She thought of fortresses built from tall sunflowers, her fright at the huge bull snake lessened at the touch of his

hand. *They rode down the hill on the frame of an old springwagon, pulled cockleburs out of the alfalfa field, picked chokecherries on the bluff.* "He's my big brother," *she whispered. Her Griffin growled at the Pelican. He dared not move.*

For purposes here, I have considerably shortened what Warren wrote back, *"I enjoyed reading your "Musing with the Pelican." Maybe you can ask him about time. What is time? Does it really exist? Is it the movement of an instant through space, or an infinite number of instants fixed in space? Is it nothing more than our method of trying to understand change? Maybe time does not exist at all. Maybe it is the only thing that does exist. What does the Pelican say about these things?"*

★★★★

Following Warren's passing in 1992, I wrote of my own sorrow. *"Hear the chime clock on my wall? Tick-tock, Tick-Tock-TICK-TOCK. Measuring-moments, measuring-hours, measuring-the-year. Measuring-TIME. What is time? Warren said it does not exist. The only time we have is past. The only time that exists is PAST! Exhaust spewing from a bus. The bus is gone, the gagging fumes remain. Sunset trails clouds of glory. The sun is gone, but its glory fills the sky. Past. Past. Warren said the only time we have is our memory of it. We measure time by events we remember. I measure my year by memory of it. What of my memory of the brother who taught me to think this way? "O God! How could you leave me the way you did? How could you leave my world? I will never again see your beloved face. I will never again hear your beloved voice."* Tears slide down my face and my heart thunders with grief.

"Sh-sh, Sissy. It's all right. All we ever had of each other was memory and we won't let that be erased. I am still part of your world."

"Do you still remember me, my brother, wherever you are?"

"Didn't I say we will not let that be erased? If I forgot you, some of my Earth experience would be lost to the Universe. And we know a thought once thought, is never lost. You were such a part of my childhood. Believe me, my sister, memory does not cease."

The future is unborn. Now is already past. Memories made, memories stored. Eternally.

I had a dream one night. I stood in the parking lot of a large shopping mall, looking toward the glass doors of the entrance. Why I was not walking in I do not know. A woman with a small, dark-haired child opened the door to go inside. The little boy, about five or six years old, turned and looked at me. My mother led him through the door, but he still looked back and reached out his hand to me. The heavy doors, transparent between us, slowly closed and cut off his hand. I sat up in bed screaming, *"O God NO! Buddy Boy!"*

"It's okay, Sissy. Don't be afraid. I leave you my hand. I know you will need it."

And again, Walt Whitman's reminder. *"I see the elder hand pressing support, I recline by the sills of the exquisite flexible doors, and mark the outlet, and mark relief and escape."*

★★★★

I took Warren's journal out of its box from time to time, read through it and typed up a page or two on my Sears Scholar typewriter, but it was painful and I put it aside again. The years passed. In 1995, I moved to San Pedro overlooking the harbor, and spent much time along the tide pools. I wrote many things, articles on ideas of philosophy, science, religion, the Universe. I wrote of time and space, of infinity. I talked to my pelican along the balustrade at Point Fermin Lighthouse where my old friend found me. His head feathers were graying, but he never failed to settle near on his one foot for the fish I brought him.

I retired from employment in 1997 and moved to Tempe, Arizona near my daughter Teri and her family. I wrote my own book. I would get Warren's Journal out, work on it a little bit, and put it away. Life kept coming at me, filling my "time" with everyday things. Margy, my other daughter, moved from California to Ohio and I spent part of every year there. When she moved back to North San Diego County, I made the trip often between Arizona and California on I-8 through Yuma. In 2004, I moved back to California, living in Riverside County. Usually I traveled the I-10, but if I wanted to deliver something between my daughters, I drove I-8 through Yuma. One trip, I took the off ramp in Yuma to see the ruin of the old Territorial Prison and the Yuma Crossing. And thought of my promise to Warren those years ago to travel US-95 paralleling the Colorado River North. I knew now that US-95 would not be the correct route to follow the Colorado River. It did run parallel, but not that close to the river itself. I would need to take a secondary road, probably the one leading north past the Marine Air Station. And I did nothing about it.

Then one day in 2008, I traveled I-8 from Tempe in my Toyota Tacoma truck, intending to stop at Los Algodones, Mexico to pick up some meds for Margy. I pulled into the rest area at Mohawk Valley, 54 miles east of Yuma.......

I heard it when I was in the restroom. The deep chuckle of a Harley Davidson FLT motorcycle. *Sweet-potata-sweet-potata-sweet-potata.* You don't mistake the sound of a Harley. Honda tried to imitate it once years ago and Harley Davidson slapped a law suit on them that said *'no-no-you-don't,'* and trademarked the sound.

I washed my hands, wondering what had ever happened to Warren's custom built Harley FLT. I knew his friend John had taken all Warren's Harleys and sold them for Conni But I think he had bought the big one for himself. Scuttlebutt was that he had moved to Texas sometime back. I walked to my Tacoma and the Harley was parked next to it. I stood stock still and very weak at the knees. Blazoned on the gas tank were the words, **"Custom Built for Warren C. Garrison by Harley Davidson."** And on the fender, **"*Clint.*"**

Should I wait to see who rode it? No. NO! I did not want to see anyone riding that motorcycle except my brother. It was customized for him and him only. I got into my Tacoma and headed out of the parking lot and down the highway toward Yuma. But five miles down the road, it caught up and passed me. I looked to see the rider then, but none was visible. Now, lots of riders lie low along the top as they ride. Today, riders of those little action figure toys that pretend to be motorcycles, ride that way. But it wouldn't be all that easy on a big vintage tour glide Harley. Still, if the man bent low he would be hard to see because of the high buddy seat. I had to assume that was it. The magnificent machine pulled on ahead until it was floating in the waving mirage a quarter mile ahead. It stayed that distance between us all the way to Yuma, then took the off ramp to the Marine Air Station. Of course, I said to myself. It belongs to a Marine. Warren would like that.

I followed. Don't ask me why. But the Harley went right past the entrance to the Air Station and on through Yuma, taking the road along the Colorado River. Still it appeared riderless. Who was I following along the Colorado River? I do not know. At the Imperial Dam, I crossed the river and detoured back to Winterhaven and I-8 to San Diego. *Let it go, Vivian.*

Warren believed time is an illusion. The only time we have is the past and our perception of it resides only in our memory of it. If that belief is true, then as long as I remember him, Warren and his big, beautiful, maroon, custom built Harley Davidson will tour the continent.

In memory of Warren C. Garrison. *Viaje con Dios, my brother. Travel with God.*

Acknowledgments

First and foremost, heartfelt thanks to Warren's wife, Kunigunde Garrison, for her untiring and loving devotion to him through the last painful days of his life. She never left his side, and under the direction of Hospice, gave him the special care he needed to honor his wish to die in his own house in his own bed. I'm sure her heart was shattered by his steady decline and no way to stop it. She wept as she said that he reminded her of the skeletal bodies of Jews she saw along the roads and in cattle cars, being driven to the death camps and ovens in Nazi Germany. Our love to you, Connie.

Primary source material is, of course, Warren's Journal. I will never be able to express my appreciation for the Internet and Google as a resource as close as my computer. Where Warren had to write to a Chamber of Commerce or tourist center for material to find data about the places he intended to travel, I simply went to iGoogle, my home page, and typed in what I wanted to know and a fantastic selection of material was at hand. Alaskajourney.com, ExploreNorth.com, flickr.com, as well as discoverpeacecountry.com, attractionscanada.com and hellobc.com, were invaluable web sites. A book that helped was "Insight Guide Alaska," from The Discovery Channel, and Los Angeles Times Archives online "Alaska" by Michael Parrish, July 2002. Also online, the University of Wyoming, with its many web sites was truly a major information source for the Oregon/ California/ Mormon Trail, much more thorough than any other available material about the Trail.

Thank you to the staff at Infinity Publishing: Mark Gregory, Gabriel Chavarria, Keith Molnar, Tim Majka, Matt Struebel,

Laura Pici, and Ivan Carter. Special thanks go to Michelle Shane, for her invaluable help in this publishing process; to Caryn Search, for expertly setting up the book; and to Chris Master, for designing the awe-inspiring cover. A special "thank you" is also given to LinDee Rochelle, an old friend, as well as my Author's Advocate.

For Warren

I-8 to Yuma

Exploring the area along Interstate 8 from Gila Bend, AZ to Yuma, geological history is varied in content and design. The Gila (Heel-ah) River runs pretty much parallel to the highway for most of the way. The miles of down-dropped Gila Trough consists of subsurface Precambrian gneiss and granite, capped by Tertiary lava flows and desert varnish. Desert varnish is made up of clay minerals mixed with wind blown desert dust deposited on metamorphic rock. Those deposits have been wet by rains that so often follow such dust storms. Over thousands of years in the alkaline environment, it darkens on the rock surfaces to a hard shiny iron-manganese coating.

Both sides of the Gila Trough are edged by vertical faults, but the floor of the plain is heavily cultivated with cotton, citrus and cattle feed. Surrounding plains are mostly volcanic lava flows. Because of the lack of gaseous material in the basalt magma, vents did not erupt, but lava gently flowed outward from these vents capping the sedimentary and metamorphic material in thin sheets and pools. This is the youngest volcanic activity in Arizona, forming some 2 million years ago. Several small cinder cones can be seen west of the town of Sentinel, that mark the center of a basalt field.

Other farm towns along I-8 are, Aztec, Tacna, and Wellton. Between them lie flat desert plains and valleys that are pretty much sand and gravel, with faulted thin ridges of mountain sub-ranges running through. Notable ranges are the Mohawk Mountains, (resembling a Mohawk haircut, really), Copper Mountains, and Gila Mountains, all made up mostly of Tertiary or Mesozoic granite and gneiss. The Muggins Mountains consist of Miocene river and lake sediments that once covered the entire area at a time when this was an inland sea. Some of these sediments at the bases of mountain ranges, contain placer gold, leading to the numerous ruins of old mining camps scattered around Southwestern Arizona.

The Lechuguilla Desert, between the Copper and Gila Mountains is fertile irrigated farmland supporting numerous citrus orchards. The Yuma Desert, between the Gila Mountains and the Colorado River is truly desert, featuring shimmering mirages and whirling dust devils in hot summers. The city of Yuma sits on the Yuma Mesa, less than 200 feet above sea level. But through the town flows the mighty Colorado River, now sadly robbed of much of its might to irrigate the flourishing valleys of agricultural endeavors. Agribusiness is not only in the United States, but along the strip of Mexico that lies between Yuma and the Gulf of California. A desalination plant just east of Yuma furnishes fresh water to Mexico, before it is put back into the Colorado to continue its journey southward.

Yuma is near the Salton Trough in California, the rift, once part of a mid-oceanic ridge, where the continent folded over creating the Gulf of California. Sand dunes to the west of the Colorado River, still retain the look of a crustal spread. The Salton Trough near Yuma cuts diagonally across Arizona between I-8 and the Mexican border. Extending northwest from I-8, it runs through the Salton Sea and is practically confluent with the San Andreas Fault.

Yuma

The best time to visit Yuma is early spring or late fall. Summer is too hot to do any exploring. Not too many years ago, my daughters, grandchildren and I spent a weekend every April and November in Yuma. Almost exactly the same distance from either Phoenix or San Diego, we got hotel rooms there, then crossed the border to Los Algodones, Mexico to shop for trinkets and lunch on really good Mexican food and drink really bad Tequila. Much fun.

But a little background on Yuma. Quechan, Cocopah and Mohave Indian tribes living along the lower Colorado River, were known as Yumans. They spoke the same language, were all agricultural people and lived peacefully together. Today, of course, they all have their own reservations. How much they pay attention to living on them is speculation. The Mohave have been moved north of I-10 above Quartsite, but still on the Colorado River. Cocopah Reservation is 12 miles south of Yuma, a small band of about 650 people. Located there, is the Heritage Art Museum. I understand they offer a Friday Night Special on the Yuma Valley Railroad along the river and a cowboy style dinner with fry bread served on the Res. Maybe I should try that sometime. The largest reservation with around 2300 people, is the Quechan. Straddling both sides of the Colorado River west of Yuma, they own the parking lot in Andrade, CA (the US side of Los Algodones, Mexico) and an RV Park there. Recently, they have built quite an elaborate Casino just off I-8. They pretty much mix with the general population. By the way, on the label in your T-shirt, you will most likely find the word Algodon. Cotton. I believe Los Algodones does not mean cotton fields, though those are nearby. I think it means Cottonwoods that line the Colorado River. These invaluable trees grow along every stream, dry creek-bed and river west of the Mississippi, creating a micro-ecosystem and nourishing the habitat.

But back to Yuma. It developed as a river town, home to soldiers, mountain men, railroaders and settlers. From 1852 until the railroad came in 1877, Colorado River paddle wheelers were the major means of transportation for supplies to the Arizona Territory, for supplies to gold miners and to the Eighth Army quartered at Fort Yuma. (It was said to be the hottest place this side of hell.) Naturally, with such a mixed variety of commerce, development and outlaws, a jail was necessary. The Yuma Territorial Prison.

It gained a reputation of being a brutal place. Not true. During its 33 years of occupation, it was considered a model prison. It had electricity before the city of Yuma did, the prisoners were treated humanely with commodious cells and acceptable food. Probably better than Maricopa County's pink underweared prisoners get today. Twenty-nine women served time in the Yuma Prison, the most famous was Pearl Hart, a stagecoach robber. Execution was forbidden. Wearing a ball and chain was the punishment for attempting to escape; though 8 men who actually made it outside the walls, were shot. Rule violators were not treated with kindness. They got to spend a spell in the "dark cell," a steel cage built inside the hill with no light or sanitation and bread and water served once a day. In 1909, this prison was abandoned for a new facility in Florence, AZ that is still there.

Yuma High School occupied the buildings from 1910 – 1914. During the Great Depression, the old prison housed homeless people who had been denied entry into California. Now it is just part of the State Historical Park, accessed from the I-8 by taking the Giss Parkway exit.

Located on the California side of the river, Fort Yuma served as military protection for settlers until the arrival of the railroad in 1883. The Quartermaster's Depot was used between 1870-1880, to bring supplies for military posts throughout the region. This was at the height of the Apache Wars. In 1884, the fort buildings were transferred to the Department of the Interior, then to the Quechan Indians. It became a Catholic boarding school until 1900. Today, beautifully restored, it is the location of St. Thomas Mission and the Quechan Indian Museum.

Yuma Crossing. This seems to have been the original site and reason for establishing any kind of settlement other than the Yumans who lived on the river. The crossing is at the point where the Gila River empties into the Colorado. The region was explored by the Spanish in 1540, coming north from the Baja along the river, via the Gulf of California. The first Spanish settlement came in 1775, led by Fr. Francisco Garces, who established a mission near this junction of rivers. Six years later, the peaceful Quechan had enough of this intrusion. The missionaries forced Catholicism on them, turned cattle and horses loose to graze on their farmland and completely destroyed their time honored way of life. They rose up and killed all the Spanish soldiers, Fr. Garces and all the men in the settlement. They did not bother the women and children who, I reckon at this point, figured they might as well live peacefully with the natives. This worked for 50 years, until Kit Carson arrived in 1829 with 2000 pounds of beaver pelts and needed to cross the river. Bingo. Yuma Crossing happened and ferry boats became the resource of the day. Carson returned on a military expedition in 1846 with Captain Phillip St. George Cook and the Mormon Battalion, to establish a wagon road across Southern Arizona Territory. Also using the crossing were Mexican and American soldiers during the Mexican War in 1846-1848. Gold seeking Forty-niners came through in the California Gold Rush. In 1877, the Colorado River was bridged for the railroad.

The settlement around the crossing was known by several names. It was Colorado City when the first post office was built in 1857. A year later, it became Arizona City and by 1866, it was officially Yuma. Lots of history for a desert city that's hotter than a piston in summertime. But it is a thriving place and growing by the day, especially since some of the Colorado River water that had been stolen for the fertile Coachella Valley in California, has been restored to Arizona ownership and farming is expanding rapidly along that side of the powerful Colorado River.

Resource material for the geology and history of the region, is taken from Halka Chronic's "Roadside Geology of Arizona," 2003, and "Arizona Ghost Towns and Mining Camps," by Phillip Varney in the Arizona Highways Books series, 1994. Copyrights are honored.

Acadiana in Louisiana

(Cajun Country)

Acadiana is made up of 22 parishes, formed by a triangle from Lake Charles in the west, to Grand Isle in the east with the apex at Pointe Coupee.

The first wave of Acadians to arrive in Louisiana after the Canadian expulsion, happened during the 1760's. They settled in an area of land nobody else wanted. Originally, Canadian Acadians were of French descent. Banished to this new land, they took up their former lifestyle. They farmed, they fished, they built self sustaining enclaves, they retained their language, and they survived. Other nationalities lived here, but Acadian culture became dominant. Intermarriage did not seem to dilute it much, but Spanish, English and African influence did eventually create some change in language that over time became uniquely Cajun. This eclectic culture remains in place because of the strong emphasis on the family ties that have kept them together throughout their history.

During the Revolutionary War, Cajun volunteers captured Baton Rouge, Mobile and Pensacola for the Colonists. From 1785 to 1790, another wave of 4,000 Acadians came to Louisiana, this time from France, and the Catholic Church began the expansion of Parishes for the Cajuns.

Acadians are credited with starting the cattle industry in the south. They had lost 100,000 head to the British in the Canadian expulsion, and cattle raising was natural in their agriculture. The first cattle brand registered in Louisiana was Cajun. This registration book, written in French, was kept in the Cajun Community until well in the 19th Century. Rice cultivation is one of their main industries. Shrimp catching and shrimp canning are primary fishing endeavors. If you see shrimp boats on the bayous, they are probably Cajun.

In 1843, Alexander Mouton was elected governor of Louisiana, the first Cajun to become a political figure. Today they hold significant political power, as well as cultural and economic power. Don't think of them as po' deep bayou folk that cook finger lickin' food and play foot stompin' fiddle. Ain't so.

As far as Evangeline is concerned, Evangeline Parish is in Acadiana and there is a town of Evangeline in Acadia Parish, but seems to be no specific monument to her in Louisiana, accepting the fact that Longfellow's poem is admittedly fiction.

Numerous Louisiana authors have written accounts over the years claiming kinship to such a story. One of the first was Sidonie de la Houssaye. In 1888, she wrote the novel, "Pouponne et Balthazar," claiming it was a family story handed down by her great grandmother. Well, Sidonie had no Acadian family connection. Ever. Her forebears were French from France.

In 1907, Felix Voorhies wrote "Acadian Reminiscences: The True Story of Evangeline," that tells of Emmeline Labiche and Louis Arceneaux who were separated during the Canadian Expulsion in 1755. Eventually the group of which Emmeline was a member, ended up in St. Martinsville, Louisiana, to be greeted by long lost friends and relatives. Louis saw Emmeline and rushed to her, taking her in his arms. But woe sad tale, by then he was married to someone else. Emmeline fell to the ground in a faint and was never well again. She spent the rest of her days in gentle madness, picking flowers and dancing along the bayous. She soon died in the new land where she had lost her lover forever.

Similar stories abound in Louisiana. One is credited to Governor Alexander Mouton, who claims Voorhies got the tale from him. Aside from Sidonie de al Houssaye, all use the names Emmeline Labiche and Louis Arceneaux. All have been told and handed down through the families by a great grandmother. There are no birth or death records of any Emmeline Labiche in Louisiana. And the Acadians were good at record keeping. A Louis Arceneaux is recorded, but born in St. James Parish, Louisiana long after the arrival of the exiles and not related to any Cajuns. (Probably named after the story?) Similar events may well have been true of many couples during the expulsion, but none can be authenticated.

It would seem, then, that the New Brunswick, Canada chapel and statue of Evangeline is nothing more than an American tourist trap with a nod to Longfellow's legendary, but fictional poem. I guess if you build it, they will come.

Source material:
Acadiancajunhistory.com,essortment.com/acadianhistory.com,carencrohighschool.org

Journal Connections by Ralph L. Garrison

Elaborating on things mentioned in Warren's Journal

The Alaska Railroad

The story of the Alaska Railroad is one of immense difficulties and hardships with seemingly insurmountable obstacles to overcome. It took the far reaching vision of bold, courageous men coupled with the dire necessity of a better means of transportation than was had at the time. Dog sleds were the only means of transporting tons of gold ore, copper, tin, platinum and coal. It was easily seen that dog sleds were hardly the feasible means of transporting ever increasing tonnage.

As to the actual history of the building of the Alaska Railroad, we must consider the few successful, as well as several abortive attempts by private individuals to furnish rail transportation for the Territory. The first was known as "The White Pass and Yukon Route," that connected the Pacific Coast at the head of the Lynn Canal with the Yukon River in Canada. It was begun shortly after the discovery of gold in the Yukon Territory and was built by Michael J. Henny. Most of the labor was supplied by men who started out to find gold, went broke, or became tired of the long, hard trail and turned aside as workers on the road.

Indeed, Mr. Henny had a most difficult task on his hands after the surveyor, E. C. Hawkins, and his assistants had finished their work. Mr. Henny was faced, not only with a scarcity of laborers, but with the rough and rugged mountains, deep gorges, and vast creeping glaciers and snow slides that kept covering his road beds and rails. Also daunting were the fierce storms one was likely to encounter in this land.

Materials were hard to get, having to be shipped from Seattle on vessels crowded with gold seekers. The Spanish-American War was demanding most of the available ships and men needed for shipping. With all these troubles, it was July 2, 1898 before the first rails were laid. By February 20, 1899, the summit of White Pass was reached by rail. Construction proceeded to Lake Bennett, arriving on July 6, 1899. July 29, 1900 saw the completion to Carcross, known at the time as Caribou Crossing. This line extends on to Whitehorse, thus connecting that city with Skagway and the Pacific Ocean.

The achievement of this supposedly impossible project broke the spell and later other companies dared the frozen North. This was the beginning of the Alaska Railroad. In 1905, another rail line, The Tanana Valley Railway, ran from Ester Junction through Fairbanks to the mouth of Cleary Creek. This line operated for a time with some success, but the need for gold ore transportation was still the dominate reason for a better railroad system.

However, far sighted individuals saw other prospects in the near future. Farming and fishing were increasing and expected to contribute to the tonnage needed for the roads to pay. The Home Railway Company and the Copper River Company fought for a right-of-way through Keystone Canyon, then both abandoned the project. Finally, in 1911, a road was constructed to Cordova and much copper and gold was shipped on this line. During this period, the United States Government began to withdraw much of Alaska's resources from the public, to make into federal preserves. With this curtailment of activities, the need for freight transportation died down. The Copper River & Northwestern Railway stopped construction of its branch to the Bering River coal fields. The Alaska Central quit with 79 miles of track laid on the way to Matanuska mines and the Fairbanks gold fields.

So many complaints were made to the federal government about the lack of interest in railroad building by the private sector, that on March 12, 1914, Congress authorized construction and operation of a government railroad in Alaska. The Alaska Engineering Commission chose the former route of the Alaska Central. That line extends for 467.6 miles from Seward to Fairbanks. The above mentioned Tanana Valley Railway was bought as part of this system.

At that point in time, World War I interfered with railroad development in Alaska. A labor force was scarce and prices rose to unheard of levels. The $35 million granted for construction, added to the original purchase price, ran out with the job unfinished. An Additional $17 million had to be provided for completion. In 1923, the 700 foot Mears Memorial Bridge was built across the Tanana River at Nenana; the final link in the Alaska Railroad. This bridge was the second longest single-span steel railroad bridge in the country. President Warren G. Harding drove the golden spike that completed the railroad in July 15, 1923. Now the Alaska Railroad accommodated both freight and passenger service.

The 1964 Good Friday Earthquake struck the rail yard and trackage around Seward and along the Turnagain Arm. Tracks were damaged by floodwaters and buckled by landslides. It took several months for full service to be restored along these lines. In 1985, the State of Alaska bought the railroad from the U. S. Government for $22.3 million, and invested over $70 million in long needed improvements and repairs.

Passenger routes of the Alaska Railroad include: The Denali Star, from Anchorage to Fairbanks and back with stops in Talkeetna and Denali State Park. This trip takes 12 hours each way as it winds through spectacular mountains and valleys. The Coastal Classic meanders south from Anchorage along Turnagain Arm to the Kenai Peninsula and eventually to Seward. The Glacier Discovery takes a short journey south of Anchorage to Whittier, then reverses direction for a stop at Grandview before returning to Anchorage the same day. The Hurricane Turn provides service to people living between Talkeetna and the Hurricane region. This area has no roads and the railway is the lifeline for residents who depend on it for transportation, food, and supplies. It is one of the last flag-stop railway routes in the United States, where passenger's can board The Hurricane Turn anywhere along the line by waving a large white cloth. The Aurora runs only in winter months on weekends between Anchorage and Fairbanks. A spur of The Alaska Railroad provides service to the Ted Stevens Anchorage International airport and is used during the summer for cruise ship connections only. The GoldStar Service provides plush, luxury seating and dining for passengers willing to pay a moderate price and private cars owned by cruise companies make use of this service. These cars are pulled behind the Alaska Railroad's own cars on most passenger routes. These trips are usually included in cruise packages.

Currently, there is a proposal to extend the railroad from Fairbanks to Delta Junction to handle agriculture and construction activity there. Planned as well, are passenger commuter services from Anchorage to Mat-Su Valley via Eagle River, and from north Anchorage to south Anchorage, but those require additional tracks to be laid because of the heavy freight schedule.

With a sometimes fragmented and colorful past, The Alaska Railroad well serves the State of Alaska from the frozen north interior to the ice-free waters of the south.

The Elbert Farm, a Different Perspective

Life on a farm in Colorado may not seem exciting to most folk, but to a small boy it proved to be a treasure island of fun and adventure. At least that is where I spent the most enjoyable years of my early life.

A few months before Pearl Harbor, my parents moved from a small town near Denver, to Elbert County. With Roosevelt's farm loan program, my dad bought a run down old place with a ramshackle house, a broken barn, and falling outbuildings. It had not been lived in for several years and it showed it. A poor, depression-ridden school teacher's family of five children; my older brother and sister, myself and twin sisters just a few months old. Like many others we were fortunate to call the clothes on our backs our own. From such an environment came my first memories. Some are sorrowful, but as is the nature of most of us, I almost entirely remember the happy ones.

I remember getting up on cold mornings. In the living room stood a coal heater, and a big Home Comfort range warmed the kitchen, but the rest of the house was unheated. In winter, Mom would call me to get up at least six times before I had the courage to jump out of bed, gather up my clothes, run to the stove and stand there shivering for several minutes before I was warm enough to dress.

Then chores. I had the responsibility of feeding the young calves. I fed the smallest ones out of a bucket. Teaching a baby calf to drink from a bucket is no easy task. To further complicate matters, from two to ten calves just a little older usually crowded in from every conceivable angle, all trying to get their heads into the pail. Sometimes, I felt like letting the poor little thing starve. To me, it didn't make sense that I had to feed the only calf in the pen that didn't want to eat. Especially when all the others pushed in so eagerly. Later, I was grateful to the man who invented a bucket with a nipple.

In the spring, crops had to be planted. At first we used draft horses to pull the farm machinery, but by the time I was big enough to operate one, we got a tractor. I liked driving that tractor. In fact, I still have it and I still like to drive it. I'd spend hours away from the house, plowing and planting. Haying time was hard work for little boys. I would go out into the fields where the hay had just been cut and raked into winnows. With a pitchfork, I'd stack it up into shocks. I never liked to shock hay. When it was cured, we hauled it to the hayloft behind the barn for winter feed. I didn't mind that so much, because I got to drive the team of horses that pulled the hayrack.

In late summer and fall, we harvested the grain crops. Most times we hired a man with a combine to do that on shares, but we still had to haul the grain to the granary. I liked harvest time. Sometimes I could ride on the tractor that pulled the combine. Once my father had the creek bed changed and I rode the bulldozer almost all day. It was great fun, but very tiring, and the next day my mother would not let me ride at all.

Once my brother bought a bicycle. It was a great big one and I was a pretty small boy. My brother ran along side and held me up, but soon he got tired of doing that and I had to do the best I could by myself. I almost wrecked his bike and nearly broke my neck, but I was determined and stayed with it. Our long driveway sloped, so I'd push the bicycle to the top, lean it against a post of the garden fence, climb aboard and take off. At first I'd go a few feet before I would topple off and crash to the ground. Sometimes I would end up on top and sometimes on the bottom. One day I fell and bent the handlebars. Then I had to ride with bent ones until my brother got new handlebars, but I finally learned how to ride it.

Probably one of the most thrilling memories I have of that period in my life, was a day a big, dirty, straggly looking black dog strayed into our yard. I'd wanted a dog for a long time, but my father did not like dogs and kept putting me off. This old fellow looked like my dream come true. I got all the food my mother would give me and fed him. He was still so hungry that I got my two little sisters and we took him to the barn and poured him some skim milk that Dad was going to feed the hogs. It was beginning to sour and that was okay for pigs, but the dog drank so much I'm surprised he survived. We took the horse currycomb and got some of the dirt and tangles out of his hair. Then he lay down and slept for hours while we sat on the ground watching him. When Dad came in from the field, he wanted to get rid of the dog, but we kids begged and Mom argued for us, so he stayed. He was always a kind and faithful friend and companion for us little ones and for Mom. He lived for many years. When he finally died, we were all grown, but I for one was far from dry-eyed when Mom wrote us of his death.

Many more wonderful things happened at the Elbert Farm. Trips to town where once in a while I could have an ice cream cone; water fights with neighbor kids when we had time to visit after Sunday dinner; playing in the hayloft of the old barn; games of hide and seek. Wood Tag and May-I? In winter, games of I-Spy and Blind Man's Bluff in the parlor; sledding on the snow on warm days; the hundreds of things children could find to do without toys, but with lots of room and a little imagination.

Like I said, lots of folk might not think it was much of a place to live, but I wouldn't trade those years for a million dollars and all the tea in China. When Dad sold the place and we moved closer to a larger town, we had more advantages and made more friends, but I was heartbroken. I still look back on that time at The Elbert Farm with fond memories, mixed emotions, and a grateful heart.

Chronicle of a Boy, a Dog, and a Tractor

It was a bright, sunny Monday morning in Mid-March, 1951. The hay wagon was loaded with household goods and miscellaneous items needed to enable the family to live in the new house to which we were moving. A coarse canvas tarpaulin overspread the wagon and its cargo in case the weather turned foul, which it did in spades. I don't remember where the tarp came from. It hadn't been around before and it wasn't new. I suppose Dad picked it up somewhere just for this trip. At the front of the load, a bed was set up for one of us to sleep while the other drove.

The trip measured well over 650 miles, and ran from our farm near Penrose, Colorado to our new farm near Brighton, Missouri. The drivers were my father and me. Our two dogs were the passengers. The motive power for the trip was our Ford tractor, *9N173376*. Loaded highway speed with the Step-up Sherman transmission was about 12 miles per hour after factoring in the up and down run of the hills. Most of the terrain averaged out about level after you figure in the loss of somewhere in the neighborhood of 5,000 feet of elevation. Dad figured it would take about three days to make the trip, driving continuously, minus the stops for gasoline and eats and other necessities. That is why the bed was set up. We meant to drive 24 hours a day. One drives, one sleeps. The tractor had headlights and Dad had rigged a wire to energize the small red tail light on the back of the wagon.

Having recently turned 15 years of age, and being a veteran of other moves from farm to farm with similar loads and same tractor, I thought myself ready for the mother of all moves. I was excited and eager to be away. That does not mean I was totally happy with the idea of leaving my native Colorado. Nevertheless, the decision to go had been made without my input and I was along for the ride, like the reason or not. The weather was mild and I was getting away from the High School where I had been the most miserable since last September.

Our first significant driving challenge was to get through traffic in Pueblo, Colorado. Beyond Pueblo, only Hutchison and Wichita, Kansas would be the larger cities. Our start was about 25 miles west of Pueblo, and that was no problem. Just open Highway 50. Dad had our route through town mapped out and he did the driving. My job was to sit atop the load and signal turns to the cars behind us. It took about 45 minutes to get through and no problems were encountered. I can imagine the problems that might come up with today's traffic. I wouldn't like to try it. In 1951, it was pretty mild.

A few miles east of Pueblo we left HWY-50 and crossed the Arkansas River in favor of Highway 96, a less traveled road than HWY-50. From that point to Hutchinson, it looked like a walk in the park. Nothing but the wide open spaces of Eastern Colorado and Western Kansas, with a few small towns along the way. Some walk in the park it turned out to be! I recall crossing the Colorado/Kansas border with some sadness.

I have a little trouble remembering just which days certain things happened, but the border crossing must have been done about the middle of the second day. Up to then and a ways beyond that point, things went as planned. A significant wind from the West came up and turned the weather somewhat colder. As the afternoon wore on, things turned bad in a hurry. By evening a full scale spring blizzard caught up with us. Western Kansas wind is a factor to be reckoned with at such times. Blowing snow blinded us and by the time we got to Leoti, Dad decided we could not make it through the night. It was simply too cold and drifting snow made driving after dark too dangerous, even for him. Dad was a tough 'get it done' person, but that weather stopped him for the night. We pulled the rig off to the side of the street across from a motel in Leoti, and checked in.

Dad's attitude toward dogs was another story, but it had an effect on what happened that night. He didn't like dogs and barely tolerated ours for the sake of us kids and Mom. Growing up on the farm, he would bring tiny piglets, baby calves or newborn foals in the kitchen for warmth, but not dogs. There was no question about bringing them into the motel with us for the night. I knew better than to ask. I'm not sure the motel managers would have known if we had. They were not policing such things that night, and given the circumstances, probably would not have minded anyway. The dogs had years of experience finding shelter during bad weather on the farm in any number of outbuildings. I supposed they would hunker down under the wagon, huddle together and survive. But this was not the farm and they had never been anywhere else.

Let me turn back a few years in time. In the spring of 1944, I read a story about a dog, possibly a Jack London book, and got a great desire to have one. Dad wouldn't hear any argument about that and I accepted the fact that I would not have a dog. The Universe had another plan. In the late summer of that year, a dog appeared at the farm. A shepherd mix, he was all black except for two brown tufts of hair on the brow above his eyes. I would guess he weighed about 65 pounds. I was immediately in love. Some controversy occurred, but Mom was on the side of us kids and in the end, the dog stayed. He was the family dog.

In 1948, my teacher at school wanted to give me a puppy. I don't remember all the discussions that happened, but I got the puppy. He was a Rat Terrier, all white except for a large brown spot that covered his left ear and eye. Now I had a dog that meant the world to me. My dog. Not the family dog. Mine. Happy Jack.

Now back to that morning in Leoti, Kansas. The initial front of the blizzard had passed and we arose to push on. When I hollered for the dogs at the wagon, the big dog came up and I put him on board. Happy Jack did not come. Dad unhitched the wagon and drove the tractor around the area, figuring Happy Jack would hear the tractor and come running. While Dad was away, I looked into the middle of the street and saw a lump under the snow. I went to my dog and picked him up in my arms and wept. I loaded him into the wagon where he reposed in frozen stillness until we got to the new farm. About the time I was putting that dear body in the wagon, Dad came back and took in the situation. He got off the tractor and hugged me and kissed my cheek. That is the first time I remember him ever kissing me. He didn't do much kissing of his kids.

I have had six dogs since then, and shed hot tears when I buried them, but no dog has ever been more loved than Happy Jack. After all these years since his tragic death, he is still deep in my heart. I suppose you could say I have a thing for dogs.

Anyone familiar with Western Kansas blizzards knows that bad ones last two to four days. However, after the front goes through, the wind moderates a little. Still, blowing and drifting snow can be an ongoing problem, especially on East/West roads. There you go; this was HWY-96 going East/West all the way across Kansas. Over 400 miles of it. I don't know how Dad lived through what he did. For the next two days he did almost all the driving. I stayed under cover and did pretty well, comforted by heavy blankets and curled up around our big black dog. It was only when Dad was thoroughly frozen and in danger of dire consequences, that he had me drive long enough for him to warm up a little. As much as he disliked dogs, I have often wondered if he may have curled up around that dog just to save his life. I have never asked and he never mentioned it.

In retrospect, I must have been in shock to a greater degree than I realized at the time. I still took my turn driving while Dad warmed up. We did not drive at night for the rest of that trip. From Leoti to Iola is still a blur to me. I vaguely remember going through Hutchinson riding shotgun and signaling traffic. Dad figured a way to bypass Wichita by leaving HWY-96 and heading east on HWY-54. I don't remember it at all. It was Friday about dusk when we pulled into Iola, our fifth day on the road. By then, weather was better and I was coming out of my daze enough to ride outside some of the time. We checked into a motel. I remember very little about eating on this trip, but that evening we went to a café near the motel. By the time we finished, it was dark. The big dog was wise enough to stay off the street and under the wagon all night. He lived until 1956 and died of old age while I was away in the Air Force.

At the motel in Iola, we went inside in the dark. A single bare light bulb hung in the ceiling over the bed. It turned on and off with a pull string. I recall that when Dad turned back the covers, we saw a dark spot on the sheet. That brought a response from Dad questioning the sanitation practices of the motel keeper, but on closer examination, the spot was caused by the shadow of a large button on the end of the pull string. What a thing to remember after a half century.

Come the morning of the 6th day, we found the weather much milder. It was still overcast, but I suspect it got up to 50° that day. What a relief. I rode outside most of time after that. And I did quite a bit of driving, now. We passed from Kansas into Missouri on HWY-54 until we reached Collins, Missouri. Then we turned south on HWY-13 until we got just past Brighton, Missouri. That would be our Post Office address for the next four and a half years.

At Brighton, we stopped at a grocery store and bought food for the next couple of days. From Brighton, Dad let me drive to the new farm. That was some significance to me. I came to be very fond of that farm yard and the precious memories formed there. The house was bare of furniture or appliances. Those were all in the wagon, and it was sundown. We gathered sticks, built a fire in the yard, roasted wieners and had a picnic. Dad didn't take to soda pop, but he had bought milk. We set up beds in the house, expecting Mom and the girls to arrive later in the night. I was asleep when they came, but I remember them coming to my bed with sympathy and tears when they learned of my loss.

The next morning, I took a shovel and accompanied by my sisters, I carried Happy Jack across the meadow about 100 yards from the house. I buried the love of my heart at the foot of an old cedar tree. If the tree is still there, I could show you the exact spot.

This has turned out to be a tale of a horribly cold few days and the death of my dog. But the tractor was there all the way, and a dear friend to me. To this day it is housed in the shop at my little farm.

★★★★

NOTE: by Vivian Zanini

A couple of years ago, Ralph's barn caught fire, probably from faulty wiring. No one was home at the time, and the barn, being full of well cured hay and straw, went up like a torch, spreading to other outbuildings. Two neighboring farm women saw the smoke and flames, called the volunteer fire department, and ran to see what they could do. Not much, until they saw the tractor shed was threatened with two tractors inside. They rushed to the old Ford, put it in neutral and physically pushed it out of the shed. Thanks to their kindness, Ralph still has the old 1945 Ford Ferguson

9N173376 Step up Sherman Transmission tractor, bought by our father at the Elbert Farm during WWII. And by the way, it still runs just fine.

A Letter to Warren, by Florence Blakey

Dear Big Brother Warren,

How grateful I am that you kept a journal of your travels the last years of your life. You were gone from home when I was so very young. My most vivid memories of you come from the time you spent with me at the farm in Pittsburg. I treasure our conversations.

Without the journal I would never have experienced your adventures or known how important it was to you to explore the routes you chose. I thank Vivian for taking the time and the huge effort it took to rewrite your journal.

Know, Warren, that I love and miss you greatly. Please give twin sister Phyllis a huge hug from me. I miss her so.

Your little sister,
Florence

Notes:

My apology to Warren for taking 18 years to honor my promise to him to ghost write his Journal. I guess it took that long for me to realize that in order to do it right, I would have to figure out how to see what he saw the way he saw it, to feel what he felt the way he felt it, and the only way I could do that was become a so-called, "chip off the old block," or "chip on his shoulder," and ride the buddy seat of the big Harley with him. He sat beside me as I wrote, and together we explored the geology and history and grandeur of North America. I learned to see his beloved Alaska as he saw it. I shivered in the cold of Nova Scotia, blistered in the heat of Death Valley in July. My God, Warren. How did you ever do that? I marveled at the Mound Builders and followed the old Oregon/California Trail. I rose and fell with the Colorado Plateau, stood on the Mogollon Rim, and listened to the old gods of the Grand Canyon. I rode with him across the Midwest, through the Ozarks, the flint hills, the prairies, the mountains. I picked chokecherries with him on the bluff at the Elbert farm. I felt the demoralization of American Indians by the US Government toward the many tribes who traveled a trail of tears from their homelands to the "Indian Nation" of Oklahoma. And then even that was taken away from some tribes and sold in lottery drawing that created the Oklahoma Land Rush during the Homestead Act.

And finally, I took back my own persona and drove the Gila Trough, I-8 to Yuma, visited the Territorial Prison, Yuma Crossing, and Fort Yuma. I pushed aside the cattails and reeds to baptize my feet in the Colorado River at Los Algodones, Mexico.

Your journal, Warren, your story. Thanks for the ride.

Sis

Order this book from:

www.buybooksontheweb.com

www.amazon.com